# FRENCH
## COUNTRY COOKING

# FRENCH
## COUNTRY COOKING

60 SIMPLE AND AUTHENTIC DISHES FOR THE TRUE TASTE OF FRANCE

CAROLE CLEMENTS
AND ELIZABETH WOLF-COHEN

southwater

This edition is published by Southwater, an imprint of Anness Publishing Ltd,
Hermes House, 88–89 Blackfriars Road, London SE1 8HA; tel. 020 7401 2077; fax 020 7633 9499

www.southwaterbooks.com; www.annesspublishing.com



UK distributor: Book Trade Services; tel. 0116 2759086; fax 0116 2759090; uksales@booktradeservices.com; exportsales@booktradeservices.com
North American distributor: National Book Network; tel. 301 459 3366; fax 301 429 5746; www.nbnbooks.com
Australian distributor: Pan Macmillan Australia; tel. 1300 135 113; fax 1300 135 103; customer.service@macmillan.com.au
New Zealand distributor: David Bateman Ltd; tel. (09) 415 7664; fax (09) 415 8892

**Publisher:** Joanna Lorenz
**Senior Editor:** Linda Fraser
**Copy Editor:** Christine Ingram
**Indexer:** Alex Corrin
**Designer:** Sheila Volpe
**Photography and Styling:** Amanda Heywood
**Food for Photography:** Elizabeth Wolf-Cohen assisted by Janet Brinkworth

The publishers would like to thank Sopexa UK for the photographs appearing on pages 1, 6, 7, 9, 19, 31, 41, 51, 63, 75, 85.



A CIP catalogue record for this book is available from the British Library.

Previously published as *French Family Cooking*

Main front cover image shows Duck Stew with Olives – for recipe, see page 61.

## NOTES

Bracketed terms are intended for American readers.

For all recipes, quantities are given in both metric and imperial measures and, where appropriate, in standard cups and spoons. Follow one set of measures, but not a mixture, because they are not interchangeable.

Standard spoon and cup measures are level. 1 tsp = 5ml, 1 tbsp = 15ml, 1 cup = 250ml/8fl oz.

Australian standard tablespoons are 20ml. Australian readers should use 3 tsp in place of 1 tbsp for measuring small quantities.

American pints are 16fl oz/2 cups. American readers should use 20fl oz/2.5 cups in place of 1 pint when measuring liquids.

Electric oven temperatures in this book are for conventional ovens. When using a fan oven, the temperature will probably need to be reduced by about 10–20°C/20–40°F. Since ovens vary, you should check with your manufacturer's instruction book for guidance.

Medium (US large) eggs are used unless otherwise stated.

# CONTENTS

# Introduction

*Country cooking is the simple, tasty food served in homes and small family restaurants throughout France. It is not without refinement, nor is it plain, but the food itself is uncontrived, uncomplicated and full of flavour. The French gastronome Curnonsky's definition of cuisine, "when things taste of themselves", is a good description of French country cooking.*

In France, the country kitchen reflects the seasons. The simpler the preparation of food is, the more flavourful the ingredients must be, and fresh seasonal ingredients are the foundation of country cooking. This fundamentally satisfying way of eating provides the opportunity to savour each vegetable and fruit as it comes to maturity, from early asparagus and strawberries to late summer pumpkins. It allows us to anticipate the enjoyment of pheasant and mallard with the arrival of the shooting season, to appreciate the taste and texture of summer shellfish and to await the first spring lamb.

Traditional recipes often combine foods that are ripe at the same time – like Brussels sprouts and chestnuts, courgettes (zucchini) and tomatoes, peaches and raspberries. The observance of nature's calendar heightens the pleasure of eating and ensures that ingredients are at their prime.

The roots of country cooking are in the land. Not so much rustic as rural, this kind of food reflects the products of the place and makes the most of them in time-honoured ways. Because country cooking is based on what produce is available locally, the repertoire varies from one part of France to another.

Think of the differences in the culinary palette between the regions of Normandy and Provence. Norman cooking relies on its renowned cream and butter, while in the south of France, olive oil is more often used. In Burgundy, beef stew is made with the local wine, but a Provençal version features tomatoes. As the ingredients change, so does the food. The common factor in all regions is the pride in local products and in preserving provincial traditions. The country kitchen is a celebration of traditional rural ways.

In rural life, nothing is wasted.

Frugality has been the inspiration for much that we appreciate in country cooking: making tarts, jams and compotes with fruit from the orchard, drying onions and garlic in the rafters of the barn, curing or smoking the meat after

*The French pride themselves on cooking with the freshest and best ingredients, like these eggs on a Breton stall (above). Shrimps netted by a fisherman (right) are likely to be eaten within a day.*

butchering a pig to provide food through the winter, preserving goose or duck in its own fat. In the country, wild mushrooms are not a luxury – they are free for the taking, as are rabbits and other furred and feathered game.

Products, such as olive oil pressed in ancient mills, local cheeses made traditionally by hand, bread baked in wood-fired ovens, butter churned from rich cream, are staples of the country table. The kitchen garden provides a constant supply of vegetables and herbs, changing throughout the year. Living close to the land in this way is something farmers take for granted and city dwellers have to cultivate, and sometimes pay a premium for, but the result is honest, wholesome and, of course, flavourful food.

Country cooking has always been the province of the people rather than of a professional elite. The development of a refined palate is not limited to those who dine regularly in starred restaurants. Universally characteristic of the French is their critical regard for food, their appreciation of fine, fresh ingredients properly prepared and cooked. This includes a recognition of the distinctiveness of products grown in certain regions and an acknowledgement of the care and attention devoted to their propagation. Such a demanding attitude is equally applicable to country food as to *haute cuisine*, perhaps more so.

Today the "real food" of France is still more likely to be found in rural areas, where people are not besieged by fast food franchises or fleeting culinary fads, and the internationalization common to capital cities has been avoided. Country inns, farmhouses offering accommodation and family-run village restaurants and hotels are bastions of honest, authentic French food. Stores selling ready-prepared food – *charcuteries*, *traiteurs* and *boulangeries* – also play a key role in carrying on the traditions of old-fashioned country cooking. Since most people have less time to cook nowadays, even those living far from urban areas, family meals at home are simpler. Increasingly, these sources of traditional country cooking are becoming essential to the preservation of regional recipes.

Like any cuisine, French country cooking evolves with new ingredients and ideas – perhaps lighter, more modern interpretations of some traditional recipes or the adoption of regional vegetables in new areas. Improved agricultural technology and transport have extended the seasons for most fresh produce and widespread travel has broadened the horizons of many people, making them open to different ways of eating. But the principles of country cooking have not changed. Fine seasonal food, prepared with a reverence for its quality, is still the foundation.

Essentially, country cooking is simple, satisfying food consumed with conviviality, and this selection of splendid authentic recipes will enable you to enjoy and share the traditions of the French country kitchen.

HUILE

# Soups and Salads

Universally satisfying, soup is a focal point of French country cooking. It is a traditional first course in farmhouse kitchens and small family bistros, providing the perfect way to enjoy seasonal produce such as young garden vegetables or stretch special ingredients such as wild mushrooms.

Salads, too, star in country fare. They make a refreshing appetizer for a robust meal in winter, or in warmer weather make an excellent light lunch. Alternatively, a simple salad of mixed leaves from the kitchen garden dressed with a light, well-balanced vinaigrette is often served after the main course, as a day without salad would seem incomplete.

# French onion soup

*Soupe à l'Oignon Gratinée*

*In France, this standard bistro fare is served so frequently, it is simply referred to as* gratinée.

Serves 6–8

*15g/½oz/1 tbsp butter*
*30ml/2 tbsp olive oil*
*4 large onions (about 675g/1½lb), thinly sliced*
*2–4 garlic cloves, finely chopped*
*5ml/1 tsp sugar*
*2.5ml/½ tsp dried thyme*
*30ml/2 tbsp plain (all-purpose) flour*
*125ml/4fl oz/½ cup dry white wine*
*2 litres/3⅓ pints/8 cups chicken or beef stock*
*30ml/2 tbsp brandy (optional)*
*6–8 thick slices French bread, toasted*
*1 garlic clove*
*340g/12oz Gruyère or Emmenthal cheese, grated*

1 ▼ In a large heavy pan or flameproof casserole, heat the butter and oil over a medium-high heat. Add the onions and cook for 10–12 minutes until they are softened and beginning to brown. Add the garlic, sugar and thyme and continue cooking over a medium heat for 30–35 minutes until the onions are well browned, stirring frequently.

2 ▲ Sprinkle over the flour and stir until well blended. Stir in the white wine and stock and bring to the boil. Skim off any foam that rises to the surface, then reduce the heat and simmer gently for 45 minutes. Stir in the brandy, if using.

3 ▲ Preheat the grill (broiler). Rub each slice of toasted French bread with the garlic clove. Place six or eight ovenproof soup bowls on a baking sheet and fill about three-quarters full with the onion soup.

4 ▲ Float a piece of toast in each bowl. Top with grated cheese, dividing it evenly, and grill (broil) about 15cm/6in from the heat for about 3–4 minutes until the cheese begins to melt and bubble.

# WILD MUSHROOM SOUP *Velouté de Champignons Sauvages*

*In France, many people pick their own wild mushrooms, taking them to a chemist to be checked before using them in all sorts of delicious dishes. The dried mushrooms bring an earthy flavour to this soup, but use 175g/6oz fresh wild mushrooms instead when available.*

SERVES 6–8

*30g/1oz dried wild mushrooms, such as morels, ceps or porcini*
*1.5 litres/2½ pints/6 cups chicken stock*
*30g/1oz/2 tbsp butter*
*2 onions, coarsely chopped*
*2 garlic cloves, chopped*
*900g/2lb button or other cultivated mushrooms, trimmed and sliced*
*2.5ml/½ tsp dried thyme*
*1.5ml/¼ tsp freshly grated nutmeg*
*30–45ml/2–3 tbsp plain (all-purpose) flour*
*125ml/4fl oz/½ cup Madeira or dry sherry*
*125ml/4fl oz/½ cup crème fraîche or sour cream*
*salt and freshly ground black pepper*
*chopped fresh chives, to garnish*

1 ▲ Put the dried mushrooms in a sieve (strainer) and rinse well under cold running water, shaking to remove as much sand as possible. Place them in a pan with 250ml/8fl oz/1 cup of the stock and bring to the boil over a medium-high heat. Remove the pan from the heat and set aside for 30–40 minutes to soak.

COOK'S TIP

Serve the soup with a little extra cream swirled on top, if you like.

2 Meanwhile, in a large heavy pan or flameproof casserole, melt the butter over a medium-high heat. Add the onions and cook for 5–7 minutes until they are well softened and just golden.

3 ▲ Stir in the garlic and fresh mushrooms and cook for 4–5 minutes until they begin to soften, then add the salt and pepper, thyme and nutmeg and sprinkle over the flour. Cook for 3–5 minutes, stirring frequently, until well blended.

4 ▲ Add the Madeira or sherry, the remaining chicken stock, the dried mushrooms and their soaking liquid and cook, covered, over a medium heat for 30–40 minutes until the mushrooms are very tender.

5 Purée the soup in batches in a blender or food processor. Strain it back into the pan, pressing firmly to force the purée through. Stir in the crème fraîche or soured cream and sprinkle with the chopped chives just before serving.

# PROVENÇAL VEGETABLE SOUP *Soupe au Pistou*

*This satisfying soup captures all the flavours of a summer in Provence. The basil and garlic purée,* pistou, *gives it extra colour and a wonderful aroma – so don't omit it.*

SERVES 6–8

*275g/10oz/$1\frac{1}{2}$ cups fresh broad (fava) beans, shelled, or 175g/6oz/$\frac{3}{4}$ cup dried haricot (navy) beans, soaked overnight*
*2.5ml/$\frac{1}{2}$ tsp dried herbes de Provence*
*2 garlic cloves, finely chopped*
*15ml/1 tbsp olive oil*
*1 onion, finely chopped*
*2 small or 1 large leek, finely sliced*
*1 celery stick, finely sliced*
*2 carrots, finely diced*
*2 small potatoes, finely diced*
*120g/4oz green beans*
*1.2 litres/2 pints/5 cups water*
*120g/4oz/1 cup shelled garden peas, fresh or frozen*
*2 small courgettes (zucchini), finely chopped*
*3 medium tomatoes, peeled, seeded and finely chopped*
*handful of spinach leaves, cut into thin ribbons*
*sprigs of fresh basil, to garnish*
FOR THE PISTOU
*1 or 2 garlic cloves, finely chopped*
*15g/$\frac{1}{2}$oz/$\frac{1}{2}$ cup (packed) basil leaves*
*60ml/4 tbsp grated Parmesan cheese*
*60 ml/4 tbsp extra virgin olive oil*

1 ▲ To make the *pistou,* put the garlic, basil and Parmesan cheese in a food processor and process until smooth, scraping down the sides once. With the machine running, slowly add the olive oil through the feed tube. Or, alternatively, pound the garlic, basil and cheese in a mortar and pestle and stir in the oil.

2 ▲ To make the soup, if using dried haricot beans, place them in a pan and cover with water. Boil vigorously for 10 minutes and drain. Place the par-boiled beans, or fresh beans if using, in a pan with the herbes de Provence and one of the garlic cloves. Add water to cover by 2.5cm/1in. Bring to the boil, reduce the heat and simmer over a medium-low heat until tender, about 10 minutes for fresh beans and about 1 hour for dried beans. Set aside in the cooking liquid.

3 ▲ Heat the oil in a large pan or flameproof casserole. Add the onion and leeks, and cook for 5 minutes, stirring occasionally, until the onion just softens.

COOK'S TIP

Both the *pistou* and the soup can be made one or two days in advance and chilled. To serve, reheat gently, stirring occasionally.

4 ▲ Add the celery, carrots and the other garlic clove and cook, covered, for 10 minutes, stirring.

5 ▲ Add the potatoes, green beans and water, then season lightly with salt and pepper. Bring to the boil, skimming any foam that rises to the surface, then reduce the heat, cover and simmer gently for 10 minutes.

6 ▲ Add the courgettes, tomatoes and peas together with the reserved beans and their cooking liquid and simmer for 25–30 minutes, or until all the vegetables are tender. Add the spinach and simmer for 5 minutes. Season the soup and swirl a spoonful of *pistou* into each bowl. Garnish with basil and serve.

# Potato Salad with Sausage

*Salade de Pommes de Terre*

*This salad is often served in bistros and cafés as a starter. Sometimes the potatoes are served on their own, simply dressed with vinaigrette and perhaps accompanied by marinated herrings.*

Serves 4

*450g/1lb small waxy potatoes*
*30–45ml/2–3 tbsp dry white wine*
*2 shallots, finely chopped*
*15ml/1 tbsp chopped fresh parsley*
*15ml/1 tbsp chopped fresh tarragon*
*175g/6oz cooked garlic sausage, such as* saucisson à l'ail
*a sprig of parsley, to garnish*

For the vinaigrette
*10ml/2 tsp Dijon mustard*
*15ml/1 tbsp tarragon vinegar or white wine vinegar*
*75ml/5 tbsp extra virgin olive oil*
*salt and freshly ground black pepper*

1 ▼ In a medium pan, cover the potatoes with cold salted water and bring to the boil. Reduce the heat to medium and simmer for 10–12 minutes until tender. Drain the potatoes and refresh under cold running water.

2 Peel the potatoes if you like or leave in their skins and cut into 6mm/¼in slices. Sprinkle with the wine and shallots.

3 ▲ To make the vinaigrette, mix the mustard and vinegar in a small bowl, then whisk in the oil, 15ml/1 tbsp at a time. Season and pour over the potatoes.

4 ▲ Add the herbs to the potatoes and toss until well mixed.

5 ▲ Slice the sausage thinly and toss with the potatoes. Season with salt and pepper to taste and serve at room temperature, garnished with a parsley sprig.

# FRISÉE LETTUCE SALAD WITH BACON *Frisée aux Lardons*

*This country-style salad is popular all over France. When they are in season, dandelion leaves often replace the endive and the salad is sometimes sprinkled with chopped hard-boiled egg.*

SERVES 4

*225g/8oz/6 cups frisée lettuce or escarole leaves*
*75–90ml/5–6 tbsp extra virgin olive oil*
*175g/6oz piece of smoked bacon, diced, or 6 thick-cut smoked bacon rashers, cut crossways into thin strips*
*55g/2oz/1 cup white bread cubes*
*1 small garlic clove, finely chopped*
*15ml/1 tbsp red wine vinegar*
*10ml/2 tsp Dijon mustard*
*salt and freshly ground black pepper*

1 ▲ Tear the lettuce into bite-size pieces and put in a salad bowl.

2 ▲ Heat 15ml/1 tbsp of the oil in a medium non-stick frying pan over a medium-low heat and add the bacon. Fry gently until well browned, stirring occasionally. Remove the bacon with a slotted spoon and drain on kitchen paper.

3 ▼ Add another 30ml/2 tbsp of oil to the pan and fry the bread cubes over a medium-high heat, turning frequently, until evenly browned. Remove the bread cubes with a slotted spoon and drain on kitchen paper. Discard any remaining fat.

4 ▲ Stir the garlic, vinegar and mustard into the pan with the remaining oil and heat until just warm, whisking to combine. Season to taste, then pour the dressing over the salad and sprinkle with the fried bacon and croûtons.

# PROVENÇAL SALAD *Salade Niçoise*

*There are probably as many versions of this salad as there are cooks in Provence. With good French bread, this regional classic makes a wonderful summer lunch or light supper.*

SERVES 4–6

*225g/8oz green beans*
*450g/1lb new potatoes, peeled and cut into 2.5cm/1in pieces*
*white wine vinegar and olive oil, for sprinkling*
*1 small romaine or round (butterhead) lettuce, washed, dried and torn into bite-size pieces*
*4 ripe plum tomatoes, quartered*
*1 small cucumber, peeled, seeded and diced*
*1 green or red (bell) pepper, thinly sliced*
*4 hard-boiled eggs, peeled and quartered*
*24 Niçoise or black olives*
*225g/8oz can tuna in brine, drained*
*55g/2oz can anchovy fillets in olive oil, drained*
*basil leaves, to garnish*
*garlic croûtons, to serve*

FOR THE ANCHOVY VINAIGRETTE

*20ml/1 heaped tbsp Dijon mustard*
*55g/2oz can anchovy fillets in olive oil, drained*
*1 garlic clove, crushed*
*60ml/4 tbsp lemon juice or white wine vinegar*
*125ml/4fl oz/½ cup sunflower oil*
*125ml/4fl oz/½ cup extra virgin olive oil*
*freshly ground black pepper*

COOK'S TIP

To make garlic croûtons, thinly slice a French stick or cut larger loaves, such as rustic country bread, into 2.5cm/1in cubes. Place the bread in a single layer on a baking sheet and bake in a 180°C/350°F/Gas 4 oven for 7–10 minutes or until golden, turning once. Rub the toast with a garlic clove and serve hot, or cool then store in an airtight container to serve at room temperature.

1 ▲ First make the anchovy vinaigrette. Place the mustard, anchovies and garlic in a bowl and blend together by pressing the garlic and anchovies against the sides of the bowl. Season generously with pepper. Using a small whisk, blend in the lemon juice or wine vinegar. Slowly whisk in the sunflower oil in a thin stream and then the olive oil, whisking until the dressing is smooth and creamy.

2 Alternatively, put all the ingredients except the oil in a food processor fitted with the metal blade and process to combine. With the machine running, slowly add the oils in a thin stream until the vinaigrette is thick and creamy.

3 ▲ Drop the French beans into a large pan of boiling water and boil for 3 minutes until tender, yet crisp. Transfer the beans to a colander with a slotted spoon, then rinse under cold running water. Drain again and set aside.

4 ▲ Add the potatoes to the same boiling water, reduce the heat and simmer for 10–15 minutes until just tender, then drain. Sprinkle with a little vinegar and olive oil and a spoonful of the vinaigrette.

5 ▲ Arrange the lettuce on a platter, top with the tomatoes, cucumber and pepper, then add the French beans and potatoes.

6 ▲ Arrange the eggs, olives, tuna and anchovies on top and garnish with the basil leaves. Drizzle with the remaining vinaigrette and serve with garlic croûtons.

# VEGETABLES AND SIDE DISHES

The colourful array of seasonal vegetables found in markets throughout France plays a key role in country cooking. Garden vegetables, woodland mushrooms, lentils and grains offer infinite variety throughout the year. The French often cook fresh young vegetables such as peas, beans and carrots quite simply – boiling or steaming them and serving with a little butter and seasoning. Some vegetables lend themselves to more elaborate presentation, and the following recipes are perfect to serve as side dishes with roast or grilled meat, poultry or game, or as part of a vegetarian meal. Whether plain or fancy, French country cooking makes the most of vegetables.

# FESTIVE BRUSSELS SPROUTS *Choux de Bruxelles Braisées*

*In this recipe Brussels sprouts are braised with chestnuts, which are very popular in France.*

SERVES 4–6

*225g/½lb chestnuts*
*125ml/4fl oz/½ cup milk*
*550g/1¼lb/4 cups small tender Brussels sprouts*
*30g/1oz/2 tbsp butter*
*1 shallot, finely chopped*
*30–45ml/2–3 tbsp dry white wine or water*

COOK'S TIP

Fresh chestnuts have a wonderful texture and flavour, but bottled or canned unsweetened whole chestnuts make an adequate substitute. They are available in delicatessens and some large supermarkets.

1 Using a small knife, score a cross in the base of each chestnut. Over a medium-high heat, bring a pan of water to the boil, drop in the chestnuts and boil for 6–8 minutes. Remove the pan from heat.

2 ▲ Using a slotted spoon, remove a few chestnuts, leaving the others immersed in water until ready to peel. Holding them in a dish towel, remove the outer shell with a knife and then peel off the inner skin.

3 Rinse the pan, return the peeled chestnuts to it and add the milk. Top up with enough water to completely cover the chestnuts. Simmer over a medium heat for 12–15 minutes until the chestnuts are just tender. Drain and set aside.

4 Remove any wilted or yellow leaves from the Brussels sprouts. Trim the root end but leave intact or the leaves will separate. Using a small knife, score a cross in the base of each sprout so they cook evenly.

5 ▲ In a large heavy frying pan, melt the butter over a medium heat. Stir in the chopped shallot and cook for 1–2 minutes until just softened, then add the Brussels sprouts and wine or water. Cook, covered, over a medium heat for 6–8 minutes, shaking the pan and stirring occasionally, adding a little more water if necessary.

6 ▲ Add the poached chestnuts and toss gently to combine, then cover and cook for 3–5 minutes more until the chestnuts and Brussels sprouts are tender.

# CAULIFLOWER CHEESE

## *Choufleur au Gratin*

*A vegetable gratin is a classic supper dish in French homes. It also makes a great accompaniment to plain roast meat or chicken. If you wish, prepare it in individual gratin dishes.*

SERVES 4–6

*450g/1lb cauliflower, broken into florets*
*45g/1½oz/3 tbsp butter*
*45g/1½oz/4 tbsp plain (all-purpose) flour*
*350ml/12fl oz/1½ cups milk*
*1 bay leaf*
*pinch of freshly grated nutmeg*
*15ml/1 tbsp Dijon mustard*
*175g/6oz/1½ cups grated Gruyère or Emmenthal cheese*
*salt and freshly ground black pepper*

1 ▲ Preheat the oven to 180°C/350°F/Gas 4. Lightly butter a large gratin dish or shallow baking dish.

2 ▲ Bring a large pan of salted water to the boil, add the cauliflower florets and cook for 6–8 minutes until just tender. Alternatively, bring water to the boil in the base of a covered steamer and steam the cauliflower over boiling water for 12–15 minutes until just tender.

3 ▲ Melt the butter in a heavy pan over a medium heat, add the flour and cook until just golden, stirring occasionally. Pour in half the milk, stirring vigorously until smooth, then stir in the remaining milk and add the bay leaf. Season with salt, pepper and nutmeg. Reduce the heat to medium-low, cover and simmer gently for about 5 minutes, stirring occasionally, then remove the pan from the heat. Discard the bay leaf, add half the cheese and stir until melted.

4 ▼ Arrange the cauliflower in the dish. Pour over the cheese sauce and sprinkle with the remaining cheese. Bake for about 20 minutes until bubbly and well browned.

VARIATIONS

If you wish, add diced ham or cooked bacon to the cauliflower before covering with the cheese sauce, or use broccoli florets in place of cauliflower.

# RICE PILAF *Riz Pilaf*

*In France the word pilaf refers to the cooking method of sautéing a food in fat before adding liquid. This method produces perfect rice every time.*

SERVES 6–8

*40g/1½oz/3 tbsp butter or 45–60ml/3–4 tbsp oil*
*1 medium onion, finely chopped*
*450g/1lb/2 cups long grain rice*
*750ml/1¼ pints/3 cups chicken stock or water*
*2.5ml/½ tsp dried thyme*
*1 small bay leaf*
*salt and freshly ground black pepper*
*15–30ml/1–2 tbsp chopped fresh parsley, dill or chives, to garnish*

**COOK'S TIP**

Once cooked, the rice will remain hot for a half an hour, tightly covered. Or, spoon into a microwave-safe bowl, cover and microwave on High (full power) for about 5 minutes until hot.

1 ▼ In a large heavy pan, melt the butter or heat the oil over a medium heat. Add the chopped onion and cook for 2–3 minutes until just softened, stirring all the time. Add the rice and cook for 1–2 minutes until the rice becomes translucent but does not begin to brown, stirring frequently.

2 ▲ Add the stock or water, dried thyme and bay leaf and season with salt and pepper. Bring to the boil over a high heat, stirring frequently. Just as the rice begins to boil, cover the surface with a round of foil or greaseproof (waxed) paper and cover the pan. Reduce the heat to very low and cook for 20 minutes (do not lift the cover or stir). Serve hot, garnished with fresh herbs.

# SAUTÉED WILD MUSHROOMS *Champignons Sauvages à la Bordelaise*

*This is a quick dish to prepare and makes an ideal accompaniment to all kinds of roast and grilled meats. Use any combination of wild or cultivated "wild" mushrooms you can find.*

SERVES 6

*900g/2lb mixed fresh wild and cultivated mushrooms, such as morels, porcini, chanterelles, oyster or shiitake*
*30ml/2 tbsp olive oil*
*30g/1oz/2 tbsp unsalted (sweet) butter*
*2 garlic cloves, finely chopped*
*3 or 4 shallots, finely chopped*
*45–60ml/3–4 tbsp chopped fresh parsley, or a mixture of fresh herbs*
*salt and freshly ground black pepper*

1 Wash and carefully dry any very dirty mushrooms. Trim the stems and cut the mushrooms into quarters or slice if very large.

2 ▲ In a large heavy frying pan, heat the oil over a medium-high heat. Add the butter and swirl to melt, then stir in the mushrooms and cook for 4–5 minutes until beginning to brown.

3 ▼ Add the garlic and shallots and cook for a further 4–5 minutes until the mushrooms are tender and any liquid given off has evaporated. Season with salt and pepper and stir in the parsley or mixed herbs.

# Garlic Mashed Potatoes *Purée de Pommes de Terre à l'Ail*

*These creamy mashed potatoes are perfect with all kinds of roast or sautéed meats – and although it seems a lot of garlic is used, the flavour is sweet and subtle when cooked in this way.*

Serves 6–8

*2 garlic bulbs, separated into cloves, unpeeled*
*120g/4oz/½ cup unsalted (sweet) butter*
*1.3kg/3lb baking potatoes*
*125–175ml/4–6fl oz/½–¾ cup milk*
*salt and white pepper*

**Cook's tip**

This recipe makes a very light, creamy purée. Use less milk to achieve a firmer purée, more for a softer purée. Be sure the milk is almost boiling or it will cool the potato mixture. Keep the potato purée warm in a bowl over simmering water.

1 Bring a small pan of water to the boil over a high heat. Add the garlic cloves and boil for 2 minutes, then drain and peel.

2 ▲ In a heavy frying pan, melt half the butter over a low heat. Add the blanched garlic cloves, then cover and cook gently for 20–25 minutes until very tender and just golden, shaking the pan and stirring occasionally. Do not allow the garlic to scorch or brown.

3 ▲ Remove the pan from the heat to cool slightly. Spoon the garlic and any butter into a blender or a food processor fitted with the metal blade and process until smooth. Tip into a small bowl, press clear film on to the surface to prevent a skin forming and set aside.

4 Peel and quarter the potatoes, place in a large pan and add enough cold water to just cover them. Salt the water generously and bring to the boil over a high heat. Cook the potatoes until tender, then drain and work through a food mill or press through a sieve (strainer) back into the pan. Return the pan to a medium heat and, using a wooden spoon, stir the potatoes for 1–2 minutes to dry out completely. Remove the pan from the heat.

5 ▲ Warm the milk over a medium-high heat until bubbles form around the edge. Gradually beat the milk, remaining butter and reserved garlic purée into the potatoes, then season with salt, if needed, and white pepper.

# FRENCH SCALLOPED POTATOES *Pommes de Terre Dauphinoise*

*These potatoes taste far richer than you would expect even with only a little cream – they are delicious with just about everything, but in France, they are nearly always served with roast lamb.*

SERVES 6

*1kg/2¼lb potatoes*
*900ml/1½ pints/3⅔ cups milk*
*pinch of freshly grated nutmeg*
*1 bay leaf*
*15–30ml/1–2 tbsp butter, softened*
*2 or 3 garlic cloves, very finely chopped*
*45–60ml/3–4 tbsp crème fraîche or whipping cream (optional)*
*salt and freshly ground black pepper*

1 ▲ Preheat the oven to 180°C/350°F/Gas 4. Cut the potatoes into fairly thin slices.

2 ▲ Put the potatoes in a large pan and pour over the milk, adding more to cover if needed. Add the salt and pepper, nutmeg and the bay leaf. Bring slowly to the boil over a medium heat and simmer for about 15 minutes until the potatoes just start to soften, but are not completely cooked, and the milk has thickened.

3 ▼ Generously butter a 36cm/14in oval gratin dish or a 2 litre/3¼ pint/8 cup shallow baking dish and sprinkle the garlic over the base.

COOK'S TIP

If cooked ahead, this dish will keep hot in a low oven for an hour or so, if necessary, without suffering; moisten the top with a little extra cream, if you like.

4 ▲ Using a slotted spoon, transfer the potatoes to the gratin or baking dish. Taste the milk and adjust the seasoning, then pour over enough of the milk to come just to the surface of the potatoes, but not cover them. Spoon a thin layer of cream over the top, or, if you prefer, add more of the thickened milk to cover.

5 Bake the potatoes for about 1 hour until the milk is absorbed and the top is a deep golden brown.

# COURGETTE AND TOMATO BAKE *Tian Provençal*

*This dish has been made for centuries in Provence and it gets its name from the shallow casserole,* tian, *in which it is traditionally cooked. In the days before home kitchens had ovens, the assembled dish was carried to the baker's to make use of the heat remaining after the bread was baked.*

SERVES 4

*15ml/1 tbsp olive oil, plus more for drizzling*
*1 large onion (about 225g/8oz), sliced*
*1 garlic clove, finely chopped*
*450g/1lb tomatoes*
*450g/1lb courgettes (zucchini)*
*5ml/1 tsp dried herbes de Provence*
*30ml/2 tbsp grated Parmesan cheese*
*salt and freshly ground black pepper*

1 Preheat the oven to 180°C/350°F/Gas 4. Heat the oil in a heavy pan over a low heat and cook the onion and garlic for about 20 minutes until soft and golden. Spread over the base of a 30cm/12in shallow baking dish.

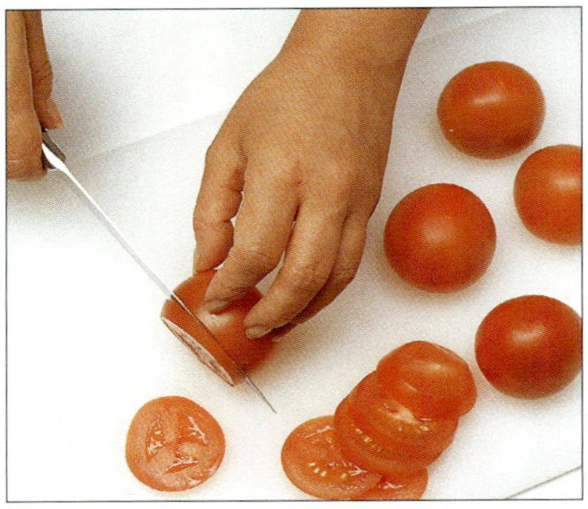

2 ▲ Cut the tomatoes crossways into 6mm/¼in thick slices. (If the tomatoes are very large, cut the slices in half.)

3 Cut the courgettes diagonally into slices about 1cm/½in thick.

4 ▼ Arrange alternating rows of courgettes and tomatoes over the onion mixture and sprinkle with herbs, cheese and salt and pepper. Drizzle with olive oil, then bake for 25 minutes until the vegetables are tender. Serve hot or warm.

# BAKED TOMATOES WITH GARLIC *Tomatoes à la Provençale*

*These tomatoes, epitomizing the flavour of Provence, are perfect with roast meat or poultry. You can prepare them a few hours ahead, then cook them while carving the roast.*

SERVES 4

*2 large tomatoes*
*45ml/3 tbsp dry breadcrumbs*
*2 garlic cloves, very finely chopped*
*30ml/2 tbsp chopped fresh parsley*
*30–45ml/2–3 tbsp olive oil*
*salt and freshly ground black pepper*
*flat leaf parsley sprigs, to garnish*

1 Preheat the oven to 220°C/425°F/Gas 7. Cut the tomatoes in half crossways and arrange them cut side up on a foil-lined baking sheet.

2 ▲ Mix together the breadcrumbs, garlic, parsley and salt and pepper and spoon over the tomato halves.

3 ▼ Drizzle generously with olive oil and bake the tomatoes at the top of the oven for about 8–10 minutes until lightly browned. Serve immediately, garnished with parsley sprigs.

# LENTILS WITH BACON

## *Lentilles Braisées aux Lardons*

*The best lentils grown in France come from Le Puy, in the Auvergne. They are very small and the colour of dark slate – look for them in delicatessens and large supermarkets.*

SERVES 6–8

*450g/1lb/2½ cups brown or green lentils, well rinsed and picked over*
*15ml/1 tbsp olive oil*
*225g/1½lb bacon, diced*
*1 onion, finely chopped*
*2 garlic cloves, finely chopped*
*2 tomatoes, peeled, seeded and chopped*
*2.5ml/½ tsp dried thyme*
*1 bay leaf*
*about 350ml/12fl oz/1½ cups beef or chicken stock*
*30–45ml/2–3 tbsp double (heavy) cream (optional)*
*salt and freshly ground black pepper*
*15–30ml/1–2 tbsp chopped fresh parsley, to garnish*

1 ▼ Put the lentils in a large pan and cover with cold water. Bring to the boil over a high heat and boil gently for 15 minutes. Drain and set aside.

2 In a heavy frying pan, heat the oil over a medium heat. Add the bacon and cook for 5–7 minutes until crisp, then transfer the bacon to a plate.

3 ▲ Stir the onion into the fat in the pan and cook for 2–3 minutes until just softened. Add the garlic and cook for 1 minute, then stir in the tomatoes, thyme, salt and pepper, bay leaf and lentils.

4 ▲ Add the stock and cover the pan. Cook over a medium-low heat for 25–45 minutes, until the lentils are just tender, stirring occasionally. Add a little more stock or water to the pan, if needed.

5 ▲ Uncover the pan and allow any excess liquid to evaporate. Add the reserved bacon, and cream, if using, and heat through for 1–2 minutes. Serve hot, with a sprinkling of chopped parsley on top.

# BRAISED RED CABBAGE

*Chou Rouge Braisé*

*The combination of red wine vinegar and sugar gives this dish a sweet, yet tart flavour. In France it is often served with game, but it is also delicious with pork, duck or cold sliced meats.*

SERVES 6–8

*30ml/2 tbsp vegetable oil*
*2 medium onions, thinly sliced*
*2 eating apples, peeled, cored and thinly sliced*
*1 head red cabbage (about 900g–1.2kg/2–2½ lb), trimmed, cored, halved and thinly sliced*
*60ml/4 tbsp red wine vinegar*
*15–30ml/1–2 tbsp sugar*
*1.5ml/¼ tsp ground cloves*
*5–10ml/1–2 tsp mustard seeds*
*55g/2oz/⅓ cup raisins or currants*
*about 125ml/4fl oz/½ cup red wine or water*
*15–30ml/1–2 tbsp redcurrant jelly (optional)*
*salt and freshly ground black pepper*

1 ▲ In a large stainless-steel pan or flameproof casserole, heat the oil over a medium heat. Add the onions and cook for 7–10 minutes until golden.

2 ▲ Stir in the apples and cook, stirring, for 2–3 minutes until they are just softened.

3 ▲ Add the cabbage, red wine vinegar, sugar, cloves, mustard seeds, raisins or currants, red wine or water and salt and pepper, stirring until well mixed. Bring to the boil over a medium-high heat, stirring occasionally.

4 ▼ Cover and cook over a medium-low heat for 35–40 minutes until the cabbage is tender and the liquid is just absorbed, stirring occasionally. Add a little more red wine or water if the pan boils dry before the cabbage is tender. Just before serving, stir in the redcurrant jelly, if using, to sweeten and glaze the cabbage.

# EGGS AND CHEESE

What could be more typical of country cooking than freshly laid farm eggs and cheese from local cows or goats? Although in France eggs are seldom eaten for breakfast, they are much enjoyed at other meals and are often paired with cheese. A soufflé is quickly prepared for a delicious first course. An omelette, quiche or cheese tart makes a satisfying supper, accompanied by a green salad. People in rural areas traditionally ate what they produced on the farm – and eggs were always handy. Nowadays we may permit ourselves this simple yet rich fare less often, but eggs, along with cheese, are an essential part of the country kitchen.

## CHEESE AND HAM CROISSANTS *Croissants au Fromage et Jambon*

*These hot croissant "sandwiches" are an upmarket version of classic café fare. They make a simple tasty lunch – try using different combinations of ham and cheese – or serve them for breakfast.*

SERVES 2

*2 large croissants*
*30g/1oz/2 tbsp butter, softened*
*Dijon mustard*
*2 slices Bayonne or Parma ham*
*55–85g/2–3oz Camembert or Brie (rind removed), sliced 6mm/¼ in thick*
*lettuce, tomatoes and chives, to serve*

1 Preheat the oven to 200°C/400°F/Gas 6. Split the croissants lengthways and spread each side with butter and a little mustard.

2 ▼ Place a piece of ham on the bottom half of each croissant, trimming to fit. Place slices of cheese on the ham and cover with the croissant tops.

3 ▲ Place the croissants on a baking sheet and cover them loosely with foil, then bake for 3–5 minutes until the cheese begins to melt. Serve with lettuce, tomatoes and chives.

## CHEESE PUFF RING *Gougère*

*This light savoury pastry comes from Burgundy, where it is traditionally served with red wine.*

SERVES 6–8

*100g/3½oz/¾ cup plain (all-purpose) flour*
*1.5ml/¼ tsp salt*
*pinch of cayenne pepper*
*pinch of freshly grated nutmeg*
*175ml/6fl oz/¾ cup water*
*85g/3oz/6 tbsp butter, cut into pieces*
*3 eggs*
*85g/3oz Gruyère cheese, cut into 6mm/¼in cubes*

1 Preheat the oven to 200°C/400°F/Gas 6. Lightly grease a baking sheet. Sift together the flour, salt, cayenne pepper and nutmeg.

### VARIATION

Stir in 15–30ml/1–2 tbsp chopped fresh parsley or chives, or chopped spring onions (scallions) before baking.

2 ▲ In a medium pan, bring the water and butter to the boil. Remove from the heat and add the dry ingredients all at once. Beat with a wooden spoon for about 1 minute until the mixture is well blended and starts to pull away from the sides of the pan.

3 Place the pan over a low heat and cook for 2 minutes, beating constantly, then remove the pan from the heat.

4 Beat the eggs together in a small bowl and then very gradually (one tablespoon at a time), beat into the mixture, beating thoroughly after each addition until the dough is smooth and shiny. It should pull away and fall slowly when dropped from a spoon – you may not need all the beaten egg. Add the cubed cheese and stir to mix well.

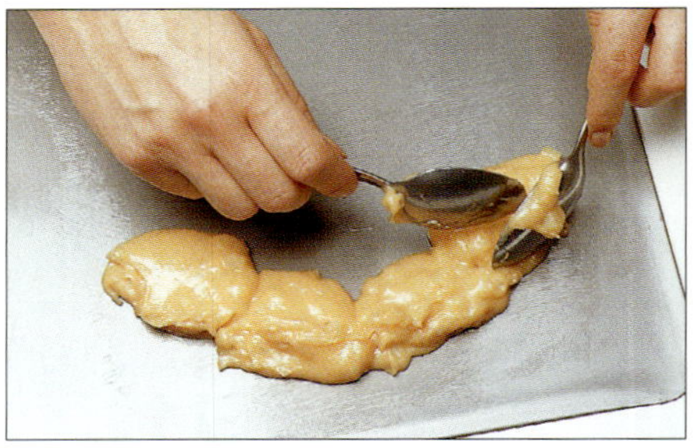

5 ▲ Using two large tablespoons, drop adjoining mounds of dough on to the baking sheet to form a 25cm/10in circle. Bake for 25–30 minutes until well browned. Cool slightly on a wire rack and serve warm.

LE F
premier quoti
à Brême

# Cheese and Onion Flan

## *Flamiche au Fromage*

*A strong-flavoured washed-rind cheese such as* Epoisses, Maroilles, *or* Livarot *is traditional in this tart but* Munster *or* Port Salut *will also produce a pleasant, if milder, result.*

### Serves 4

*15g/½oz/1 tbsp butter*
*1 onion, halved and sliced*
*2 eggs*
*250ml/8fl oz/1 cup single (light) cream*
*225g/8oz strong-flavoured semi-soft cheese, rind removed (about 175g/6oz without rind), sliced*
*salt and freshly ground black pepper*
*lettuce and parsley leaves, to serve*

For the yeast dough

*10ml/2 tsp active dry yeast*
*125ml/4fl oz/½ cup milk*
*5ml/1 tsp sugar*
*1 egg yolk*
*225g/8oz/1¾ cups plain (all-purpose) flour, plus more for kneading*
*2.5ml/½ tsp salt*
*55g/2oz/4 tbsp butter, softened*

1 First make the yeast dough. Place the yeast in a small bowl. Warm the milk in a pan until it is at body temperature and stir into the yeast with the sugar, stirring until the yeast has dissolved. Leave the yeast mixture to stand for 3 minutes, then beat in the egg yolk.

2 Put the flour and salt in a food processor fitted with the metal blade and pulse twice to combine. With the machine running, slowly pour in the yeast mixture. Scrape down the sides and continue processing for 2–3 minutes. Add the butter and process for another 30 seconds.

3 Transfer the dough to a lightly oiled bowl. Cover with a cloth and allow to rise in a warm place for about 1 hour until doubled in bulk, then punch down.

4 Roll the dough into a 30cm/12in round on a lightly floured surface. Use to line a 23cm/9in flan tin (quiche pan) or dish. Trim any overhanging dough so that it is about 3mm/⅛in outside the rim of the tin or dish. Set aside and leave to rise again for about ½ hour, or until puffy.

5 ▲ Meanwhile, melt the butter in a heavy pan and fry the onion, covered, over a medium-low heat for about 15 minutes, until softened, stirring occasionally. Uncover the pan and continue cooking, stirring frequently, until the onion is very soft and caramelized.

6 Preheat the oven to 180°C/350°F/Gas 4. Beat together the eggs and cream. Season with salt and pepper and stir in the cooked onion.

7 ▲ Arrange the cheese on the base of the dough. Pour over the egg mixture and bake for 30–35 minutes until the bread base is golden and the centre just set. Cool on a wire rack before serving hot or warm with lettuce and parsley leaves.

# CHEESE AND BACON QUICHE *Quiche Savoyarde*

*Gruyère is probably the most important French cheese for cooking. Made in the rugged Alpine dairy country of the Savoie, it is firm and has a rich nutty flavour.*

SERVES 6–8

*340g/12oz shortcrust pastry*
*15ml/1 tbsp Dijon mustard*
*175g/6oz/6 rindless streaky (fatty) bacon rashers (strips), chopped*
*1 onion, chopped*
*3 eggs*
*350ml/12fl oz/1½ cups single (light) cream*
*150g/5oz Gruyère cheese, diced*
*salt and freshly ground black pepper*
*fresh parsley, to garnish*

1 ▲ Preheat the oven to 200°C/400°F/Gas 6. Roll out the pastry thinly and use to line a 23cm/9in flan tin (quiche pan). Prick the base of the pastry case and line with foil. Fill with baking beans and bake for 15 minutes. Remove the foil and beans, brush the case with mustard and bake for a further 5 minutes, then transfer to a wire rack. Reduce the oven to 180°C/350°F/Gas 4.

2 ▲ In a frying pan, cook the bacon over a medium heat until crisp and browned, stirring occasionally.

3 ▲ Remove the bacon with a slotted spoon and drain on kitchen paper. Pour off most of the fat from the pan, add the onion and cook over a medium-low heat for about 15 minutes until very soft and golden, stirring occasionally.

4 Beat together the eggs and cream and season with salt and pepper.

5 ▼ Sprinkle half the cheese over the pastry, spread the onion over the cheese and add the bacon, then top with the remaining cheese.

6 Pour on the egg mixture and bake for 35–45 minutes until set. Transfer to a wire rack to cool slightly. Serve warm, garnished with parsley.

# ALSATIAN LEEK AND ONION TARTLETS *Tartlettes Alsaciennes*

*The savoury filling in these tartlets is traditional in north-east France where many types of quiche are popular. Baking in individual tins makes for easier serving and looks attractive too.*

SERVES 6

*30g/1oz/2 tbsp butter, cut into 8 pieces*
*1 onion, thinly sliced*
*2.5ml/½ tsp dried thyme*
*450g/1lb leeks, thinly sliced*
*55g/2 oz/5 tbsp grated Gruyère or Emmenthal cheese*
*3 eggs*
*300ml/½ pint/1¼ cups single (light) cream*
*pinch of freshly grated nutmeg*
*lettuce and parsley leaves and cherry tomatoes, to serve*

FOR THE PASTRY

*175g/6oz/1⅓ cup plain (all-purpose) flour*
*85g/3oz/6 tbsp cold butter*
*1 egg yolk*
*30–45ml/2–3 tbsp cold water*
*2.5ml/½ tsp salt*

1 To make the pastry, sift the flour into a bowl and add the butter. Using your fingertips or a pastry blender, rub or cut the butter into the flour until the mixture resembles fine breadcrumbs.

2 ▲ Make a well in the flour mixture. In a small bowl, beat together the egg yolk, water and salt. Pour into the well and, using a fork, lightly combine the flour and liquid until the dough begins to stick together. Form into a flattened ball. Wrap and chill for 30 minutes.

3 ▲ Lightly butter six 10cm/4in tartlet tins (muffin pans). On a lightly floured surface, roll out the dough until about 3mm/⅛in thick, then using a 12.5cm/5in cutter, cut as many rounds as possible. Gently ease the pastry rounds into the tins, pressing the pastry firmly into the base and sides. Reroll the trimmings and line the remaining tins. Prick the bases and chill for 30 minutes.

4 ▲ Preheat the oven to 190°C/375°F/Gas 5. Line the pastry cases with foil and fill with baking beans. Place them on a baking sheet and bake for 6–8 minutes until the pastry edges are golden. Lift out the foil and beans and bake the pastry cases for a further 2 minutes until the bases appear dry. Transfer to a wire rack to cool. Reduce the oven to 180°C/350°F/Gas 4.

5 ▲ In a large frying pan, melt the butter over a medium heat, then add the onion and thyme and cook for 3–5 minutes until the onion is just softened, stirring frequently. Add the leeks and cook for 10–12 minutes until they are soft and tender. Divide the mixture among the pastry cases and sprinkle each with cheese, dividing it evenly.

6 ▲ In a medium bowl, beat together the eggs, cream, nutmeg and salt and pepper. Place the pastry cases on a baking sheet and pour in the egg mixture. Bake for 15–20 minutes until set and golden. Transfer the tartlets to a wire rack to cool slightly, then remove them from the tins and serve warm or at room temperature with lettuce and parsley leaves and cherry tomatoes.

# TWICE-BAKED SOUFFLÉS

## *Soufflés Renversés*

*These little soufflés are served upside-down! They are remarkably easy to make and can be prepared up to a day in advance, then reheated in the sauce – perfect for easy entertaining.*

SERVES 6

*20g/¾oz/1½ tbsp butter*
*30ml/2 tbsp plain (all-purpose) flour*
*150ml/¼ pint/⅔ cup milk*
*1 small bay leaf*
*freshly grated nutmeg*
*2 eggs, separated, plus 1 egg white, at room temperature*
*85g/3oz/⅔ cup grated Gruyère cheese*
*1.5ml/¼ tsp cream of tartar*
*salt and freshly ground black pepper*
*FOR THE TOMATO CREAM SAUCE*
*300ml/½ pint/1¼ cups whipping cream*
*10ml/2 tsp tomato purée (paste)*
*1 ripe tomato, peeled, seeded and finely diced*
*salt and cayenne pepper*

1 Preheat the oven to 190°C/375°F/Gas 5. Generously butter six 175ml/6fl oz/¾ cup ramekins or dariole moulds, then line the bases with buttered baking parchment.

2 ▲ In a heavy pan over a medium heat, melt the butter, stir in the flour and cook until just golden, stirring occasionally. Pour in about half the milk, whisking vigorously until smooth, then whisk in the remaining milk and add the bay leaf. Season with a little salt and plenty of pepper and nutmeg. Bring to the boil and cook, stirring constantly, for about 1 minute.

3 ▲ Remove the sauce from the heat and discard the bay leaf. Beat the egg yolks, one at a time, into the hot sauce, then stir in the cheese until it is melted. Set aside.

4 In a large, clean greasefree bowl, whisk the egg whites slowly until they become frothy. Add the cream of tartar, then increase the speed and whisk until they form peaks that just flop over at the top.

5 ▲ Whisk a spoonful of beaten egg whites into the cheese sauce to lighten it. Pour the cheese sauce over the remaining whites. Using a rubber spatula or large metal spoon, gently fold the sauce into the whites.

COOK'S TIP

If making ahead, cool the cooked soufflés, then cover and chill. Bring the soufflés back to room temperature before baking.

6 ▲ Spoon the soufflé mixture into the prepared dishes, filling them about three-quarters full. Put the dishes in a shallow baking dish and pour in boiling water to come halfway up the sides of the dishes. Bake for about 18 minutes until puffed and golden brown. Let the soufflés cool in the dishes long enough to deflate.

7 ▲ To make the sauce, bring the cream just to the boil in a small pan. Reduce the heat, stir in the tomato purée and diced tomato and cook for 2–3 minutes. Season with salt and cayenne pepper. Spoon a thin layer of sauce into a gratin dish just large enough to hold the soufflés. Run a knife around the edge of the soufflés and invert to unmould. Remove the lining paper if necessary. Pour the remaining sauce over the soufflés and bake for 12–15 minutes until well browned.

Farine

# FISH AND SHELLFISH

The fervour for freshness and simplicity that characterizes French country cooking makes it perfect for fish and shellfish. With vast areas of coastline on two oceans, France has a superb array of seafood, changing with the seasons and the location, on offer in weekly markets in all its regions. Local fishermen sell the catch from the quayside or the beach all along the Mediterranean, where it is simmered in fish stews or simply baked or grilled. In Normandy and Brittany, mussels and scallops are gathered fresh from the sea and steamed or sautéed in butter. Uncomplicated country cooking highlights the fresh briney aromas and delicate flavours of almost all fish and shellfish.

# Scallops with Mushrooms *Coquilles Saint Jacques au Gratin*

*This dish has been a classic on bistro menus since Hemingway's days in Paris – it makes an appealing appetizer, or serve it as a rich and elegant main course.*

Serves 2–4

*250ml/8fl oz/1 cup dry white wine*
*125ml/4fl oz/½ cup water*
*2 shallots, finely chopped*
*1 bay leaf*
*450g/1lb shelled scallops, rinsed*
*40g/1½oz/3 tbsp butter*
*40g/1½oz/3 tbsp plain (all-purpose) flour*
*90ml/6 tbsp whipping cream*
*freshly grated nutmeg*
*175g/6oz mushrooms, thinly sliced*
*45–60ml/3–4 tbsp dry breadcrumbs*
*salt and freshly ground black pepper*

1 ▼ Combine the wine, water, shallots and bay leaf in a medium pan. Bring to the boil, then reduce the heat to medium-low and simmer for 10 minutes. Add the scallops, cover and simmer for 3–4 minutes until they are opaque.

2 Remove the scallops from the cooking liquid with a slotted spoon and boil the liquid until reduced to 175ml/6fl oz. Strain the liquid.

3 ▲ Carefully pull off the tough muscle from the side of the scallops and discard. Slice the scallops in half crossways.

4 ▲ Melt 30g/1oz/2 tbsp of the butter in a heavy pan over a medium-high heat. Stir in the flour and cook for 2 minutes. Add the reserved cooking liquid, whisking vigorously until smooth, then whisk in the cream and season with salt, pepper and nutmeg. Reduce the heat to low and simmer for 10 minutes, stirring frequently.

5 Melt the remaining butter in a frying pan over a medium-high heat. Add the mushrooms and cook for about 5 minutes until lightly browned, stirring frequently. Stir the mushrooms into the sauce.

6 Preheat the grill (broiler). Add the scallops to the sauce and adjust the seasoning. Spoon the mixture into four individual gratin dishes, large scallop shells or a flameproof baking dish and sprinkle with breadcrumbs. Grill (broil) until brown and bubbly.

# Mussels Steamed in White Wine — *Moules Marinières*

*This is the best and easiest way to serve the small tender mussels,* bouchots, *which are farmed along much of the French coast line. In Normandy the local sparkling dry cider is often used instead of white wine. Serve with plenty of crusty French bread to dip in the juices.*

Serves 4

*2kg/4½lb mussels*
*300ml/½ pint/1¼ cups dry white wine*
*4–6 large shallots, finely chopped*
*bouquet garni*
*freshly ground black pepper*

1 ▲ Discard any broken mussels and those with open shells that refuse to close when tapped. Under cold running water, scrape the mussel shells with a knife to remove any barnacles and pull out the stringy "beards". Soak the mussels in several changes of cold water for at least 1 hour.

2 ▲ In a large heavy flameproof casserole combine the wine, shallots, bouquet garni and plenty of pepper. Bring to the boil over a medium-high heat and cook for 2 minutes.

3 ▲ Add the mussels and cook, tightly covered, for 5 minutes, or until the mussels open, shaking and tossing the pan occasionally. Discard any mussels that do not open.

4 Using a slotted spoon, divide the mussels among warmed soup plates. Tilt the casserole a little and hold for a few seconds to allow any sand to settle to the bottom.

5 Spoon or pour the cooking liquid over the mussels, dividing it evenly, then serve immediately.

### Variation

For Mussels with Cream Sauce *(Moules à la Crème),* cook as above, but transfer the mussels to a warmed bowl and cover to keep warm. Strain the cooking liquid through a muslin-lined sieve (strainer) into a large pan and boil for about 7–10 minutes to reduce by half. Stir in 90ml/6 tbsp whipping cream and 30ml/2 tbsp chopped parsley, then add the mussels. Cook for about 1 minute more to reheat the mussels.

# MEDITERRANEAN FISH STEW *Bouillabaisse*

*Different variations of* bouillabaisse *abound along the Mediterranean coast – every village seems to have its own version – and almost any combination of fish and shellfish can be used.*

SERVES 8

*2.5kg/6lb white fish, such as sea bass, snapper or monkfish, filleted and skinned (choose thick fish)*
*45ml/3 tbsp extra virgin olive oil*
*grated rind of 1 orange*
*1 garlic clove, very finely chopped*
*pinch of saffron threads*
*30ml/2 tbsp pastis (anise liqueur)*
*1 small fennel bulb, finely chopped*
*1 large onion, finely chopped*
*225g/½lb small new potatoes, sliced*
*900g/2lb large raw Mediterranean prawns (shrimp), peeled*
*croûtons, to serve*

FOR THE STOCK

*1–1.3kg/2–3lb fish heads, bones and trimmings*
*30ml/2 tbsp olive oil*
*2 leeks, sliced*
*1 onion, halved and sliced*
*1 red (bell) pepper, cored and sliced*
*675g/1½lb ripe tomatoes, cored and quartered*
*4 garlic cloves, sliced*
*bouquet garni*
*rind of ½ orange, removed with a vegetable peeler*
*2 or 3 pinches saffron threads*

FOR THE ROUILLE

*30g/1oz/⅔ cup soft white breadcrumbs*
*1 or 2 garlic cloves, very finely chopped*
*½ red (bell) pepper, roasted*
*5ml/1 tsp tomato purée (paste)*
*125ml/4fl oz/½ cup extra virgin olive oil*

COOK'S TIP

Be sure to ask at the fish counter for the heads, tails and trimmings from your fish fillets and avoid strong-flavoured oily fish, such as mackerel. To reduce last-minute work, you can make the *rouille*, croûtons and stock early in the day, while the fish marinates.

1 ▲ Cut the fish fillets into serving pieces, then trim off any thin parts and reserve for the stock. Put the fish in a bowl with 30ml/2 tbsp of the olive oil, the orange rind, garlic, saffron and pastis. Turn to coat well, cover and chill.

2 ▲ To make the stock, rinse the fish heads and bones under cold running water. Heat the olive oil in a large, preferably stainless steel, pan or flameproof casserole. Add the leeks, onion and pepper and cook over a medium heat for about 5 minutes until the onion starts to soften, stirring occasionally. Add the fish heads, bones and trimmings, with any heads or shells from the prawns. Then add the tomatoes, garlic, bouquet garni, orange rind, saffron and enough cold water to cover the ingredients by 2.5cm/1in.

3 Bring to the boil, skimming any foam that rises to the surface, then reduce the heat and simmer, covered, for ½ hour, skimming once or twice more. Strain the stock.

4 ▲ To make the *rouille,* soak the breadcrumbs in water then squeeze dry. Put the breadcrumbs in a food processor with the garlic, roasted red pepper and tomato purée and process until smooth. With the machine running, slowly pour the oil through the feed tube, scraping down the sides once or twice.

5 ▲ To finish the bouillabaise, heat the remaining 15ml/1 tbsp of olive oil in a wide flameproof casserole over a medium heat. Cook the fennel and onion for about 5 minutes until the onion just softens, then add the stock. Bring to the boil, add the potatoes and cook for 5–7 minutes. Reduce the heat to medium and add the fish, starting with the thickest pieces and adding the thinner ones after 2 or 3 minutes. Add the prawns and continue simmering gently until all the fish and shellfish is cooked.

6 Transfer the fish, shellfish and potatoes to a heated tureen or soup plates. Adjust the seasoning and ladle the soup over. Serve with croûtons spread with *rouille*.

PASTIS

# POTATO-TOPPED BAKED FISH *Poisson au Suquet*

*This informal fish bake is said to have originated with the fishermen on the Côte d'Azur who would cook the remains of their catch for lunch in the still-warm baker's oven.*

SERVES 4

*3 medium potatoes*
*2 onions, halved and sliced*
*30ml/2 tbsp olive oil, plus more for drizzling*
*2 garlic cloves, very finely chopped*
*675g/1½lb thick skinless fish fillets, such as turbot or sea bass*
*1 bay leaf*
*1 thyme sprig*
*3 tomatoes, peeled and thinly sliced*
*30ml/2 tbsp orange juice*
*60ml/4 tbsp dry white wine*
*2.5ml/½ tsp saffron threads, steeped in 60ml/4 tbsp boiling water*
*salt and freshly ground black pepper*

1 ▼ Cook the potatoes in boiling salted water for 15 minutes, then drain. When the potatoes are cool enough to handle, peel off the skins and slice them thinly.

2 ▲ Meanwhile, in a heavy frying pan, fry the onions in the oil over a medium-low heat for about 10 minutes, stirring frequently. Add the garlic and continue cooking for a few minutes until the onions are soft and golden.

3 Preheat the oven to 190°C/375°F/Gas 5. Layer half the potato slices in a 2 litre/3⅓ pint/8 cup baking dish. Cover with half the onions. Season with salt and pepper.

4 ▲ Place the fish fillets on top of the vegetables and tuck in the herbs between them. Top with the tomato slices and then the remaining onions and potatoes.

5 Pour over the orange juice, wine and saffron liquid, season with salt and pepper and drizzle a little extra olive oil on top. Bake uncovered for about 30 minutes until the potatoes are tender and the fish is cooked.

# COD WITH LENTILS AND LEEKS *Morue aux Lentilles et Poireaux*

*This unusual dish, discovered in a Parisian* charcuterie, *is great for entertaining. You can cook the vegetables ahead of time and let it bake while the first course is served.*

SERVES 4

*150g/5oz/1 cup green lentils*
*1 bay leaf*
*1 garlic clove, finely chopped*
*grated rind of 1 orange*
*grated rind of 1 lemon*
*pinch of ground cumin*
*15g/½oz/1 tbsp butter*
*450g/1lb leeks, thinly sliced or cut into julienne strips*
*300ml/½ pint/1¼ cups whipping cream*
*15ml/1 tbsp lemon juice, or to taste*
*750g/1¾lb thick skinless cod or haddock fillets*
*salt and freshly ground black pepper*

1 Rinse the lentils and put them in a large pan with the bay leaf and garlic. Add enough water to cover by 5cm/2in. Bring to the boil, and boil gently for 10 minutes, then reduce the heat and simmer for a further 15–30 minutes until the lentils are just tender.

2 ▲ Drain the lentils and discard the bay leaf, then stir in half the orange rind and all the lemon rind and season with ground cumin and salt and pepper. Transfer to a shallow baking dish or gratin dish. Preheat the oven to 190°C/375°F/Gas 5.

3 ▼ Melt the butter in a medium pan over a medium heat, then add the leeks and cook, stirring frequently, until just softened. Add 225ml/8fl oz/1 cup of the cream and the remaining orange rind and cook gently for 15–20 minutes until the leeks are completely soft and the cream has thickened slightly. Stir in the lemon juice and season with salt and plenty of pepper.

4 ▲ Cut the fish into four pieces, then, with your fingertips, locate and pull out any small bones. Season the fish with salt and pepper, place on top of the lentil mixture and press down slightly into the lentils. Cover each piece of fish with quarter of the leek mixture and pour 15ml/1 tbsp of the remaining cream over each. Bake for about 30 minutes until the fish is cooked through and the topping is lightly golden.

# SAUTÉED SCALLOPS *Coquilles Saint Jacques Meunières*

*Scallops go well with all sorts of sauces, but simple cooking is the best way to enjoy their flavour.*

SERVES 2

*450g/1lb shelled scallops*
*30g/1oz/2 tbsp butter*
*30ml/2 tbsp dry white vermouth*
*15ml/1 tbsp finely chopped fresh parsley*
*salt and freshly ground black pepper*

1 Rinse the scallops under cold running water to remove any sand or grit and pat dry using kitchen paper. Season them lightly with salt and pepper.

2 ▼ In a frying pan large enough to hold the scallops in one layer, heat half the butter until it begins to colour. Sauté the scallops for 3–5 minutes, turning, until golden brown on both sides and just firm to the touch. Remove to a serving platter and cover to keep warm.

3 ▲ Add the vermouth to the hot frying pan, swirl in the remaining butter, add the parsley and pour the sauce over the scallops. Serve immediately.

# GARLICKY SCALLOPS AND PRAWNS *Fruits de Mer à la Provençale*

*Scallops and prawns are found all along the Atlantic and Mediterranean coasts of France and are enjoyed in every region. This method of cooking is typical in Provence.*

SERVES 2–4

*6 large shelled scallops*
*6–8 large raw prawns (shrimp), peeled*
*plain (all-purpose) flour, for dusting*
*30–45ml/2–3 tbsp olive oil*
*1 garlic clove, finely chopped*
*15ml/1 tbsp chopped fresh basil*
*30–45ml/2–3 tbsp lemon juice*
*salt and freshly ground black pepper*

VARIATION

To make a richer sauce, transfer the cooked scallops and prawns (shrimp) to a warmed plate. Pour in 60ml/4 tbsp dry white wine and boil to reduce by half. Add 15g/½oz/1 tbsp unsalted (sweet) butter, whisking until it melts and the sauce thickens slightly. Pour over the scallops and prawns.

1 ▼ Rinse the scallops under cold running water to remove any sand or grit. Pat them dry using kitchen paper and cut in half crossways. Season the scallops and prawns with salt and pepper and dust lightly with flour, shaking off excess.

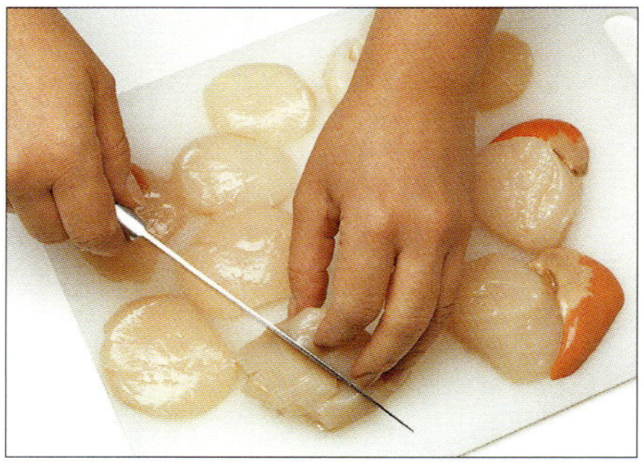

2 Heat the oil in a large frying pan over a high heat and add the scallops and prawns.

3 ▲ Reduce heat to medium-high and cook for 2 minutes, then turn the scallops and prawns and add the garlic and basil, shaking the pan to distribute them evenly. Cook for a further 2 minutes until golden and just firm to the touch. Sprinkle over the lemon juice and toss to blend.

# POULTRY AND GAME

Country cooking comes into its own with barnyard birds and woodland and water fowl. Poultry, especially chicken, is not only one of the most versatile foods, it is plentiful and relatively inexpensive, although that has not always been the case. At a country market, you can usually find a large selection of fresh, free-range chickens, ducks, guinea fowl and game birds in season, perhaps still with their plumage. Hunting is a popular autumn pastime in France, and game, both wild and reared, is widely enjoyed. Favourite regional recipes, whether quickly sautéed with farm-fresh produce or long simmered for rich flavour, celebrate poultry and game.

# Chicken with Morels *Suprêmes de Volaille Farcies aux Morilles*

*Morels are among the most tasty dried mushrooms and, although expensive, a little goes a long way. Of course, you can use fresh morels (about 275g/10oz) in place of the dried ones, or substitute chanterelles, shiitake or oyster mushrooms.*

Serves 4

*45g/1½oz dried morel mushrooms*
*250ml/8fl oz/1 cup chicken stock*
*55g/2oz/4 tbsp butter*
*5 or 6 shallots, thinly sliced*
*100g/3½oz button (white) mushrooms, thinly sliced*
*1.5ml/¼ tsp dried thyme*
*175ml/6fl oz/¾ cup double (heavy) or whipping cream*
*30–45ml/2–3 tbsp brandy*
*4 skinless boneless chicken breasts (about 200g/7oz each)*
*15ml/1 tbsp vegetable oil*
*175ml/6fl oz/¾ cup Champagne or dry sparkling wine*
*salt and freshly ground black pepper*

1 ▲ Put the morels in a strainer and rinse well under cold running water, shaking to remove as much sand as possible. Put them in a pan with the stock and bring to the boil over a medium-high heat. Remove the pan from the heat and leave to stand for 1 hour.

2 Remove the morels from the cooking liquid and strain the liquid through a very fine sieve or muslin-lined strainer and reserve for the sauce. Reserve a few whole morels and slice the rest.

3 ▲ Melt half the butter in a frying pan over a medium heat. Add the shallots and cook for 2 minutes until softened, then add the morels and mushrooms and cook, stirring frequently, for 2–3 minutes. Season and add the thyme, brandy and 100ml/3½fl oz/⅓ cup of the cream. Reduce the heat and simmer gently for 10–12 minutes until any liquid has evaporated, stirring occasionally. Remove the morel mixture from the pan and set aside.

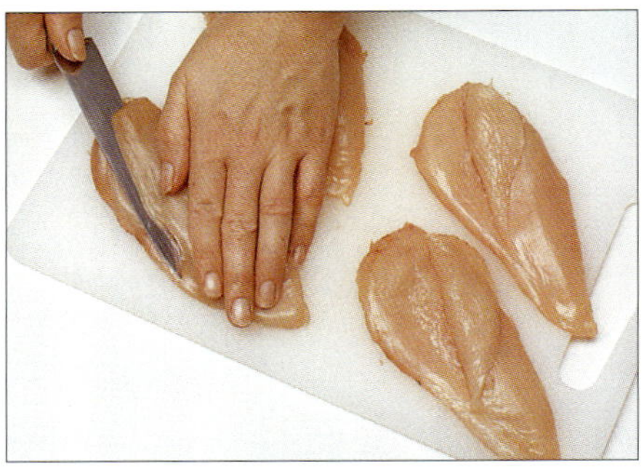

4 ▲ Pull the fillets (the finger-shaped piece on the underside) off the chicken breasts and reserve for another use. Make a pocket in each chicken breast by cutting a slit along the thicker edge, taking care not to cut all the way through.

5 Using a small spoon, fill each pocket with one-quarter of the mushroom mixture then close with a cocktail stick (toothpick) if needed.

6 ▲ Melt the remaining butter with the oil in a heavy frying pan over a medium-high heat and cook the chicken breasts on one side for 6–8 minutes until golden. Transfer the chicken breasts to a plate. Add the Champagne or sparkling wine to the pan and boil to reduce by half. Add the strained morel cooking liquid and boil to reduce by half again.

7 ▲ Add the remaining cream and cook over a medium heat for about 2–3 minutes until the sauce thickens slightly and coats the back of a spoon. Adjust the seasoning. Return the chicken to the pan with any accumulated juices and the reserved whole morels and simmer for 3–5 minutes over a medium-low heat until the chicken breasts are hot and the juices run clear when the meat is pierced with a knife.

# CHICKEN WITH GARLIC *Poulet à l'Ail*

*Use fresh new season's garlic if you can find it – there's no need to peel the cloves if the skin is not papery. In France, sometimes the cooked garlic cloves are spread on toasted country bread.*

SERVES 8

*2kg/4½lb chicken pieces*
*1 large onion, halved and sliced*
*3 large garlic bulbs (about 200g/7oz), separated into cloves and peeled*
*150ml/¼ pint/⅔ cup dry white wine*
*175ml/6fl oz/¾ cup chicken stock*
*4–5 thyme sprigs, or 2.5ml/½ tsp dried thyme*
*1 small rosemary sprig, or a pinch of ground rosemary*
*1 bay leaf*
*salt and freshly ground black pepper*

1 Preheat the oven to 190°C/375°F/Gas 5. Pat the chicken pieces dry and season with salt and pepper.

2 ▼ Put the chicken, skin side down in a large flameproof casserole and set over a medium-high heat. Turn frequently and transfer the chicken to a plate when browned. Cook in batches if necessary and pour off the fat after browning.

3 ▲ Add the onion and garlic to the casserole and cook over a medium-low heat, covered, until lightly browned, stirring frequently.

4 Add the wine to the casserole, bring to the boil and return the chicken to the casserole. Add the stock and herbs and bring back to the boil. Cover and transfer to the oven. Cook for 25 minutes, or until the chicken is tender and the juices run clear when the thickest part of the thigh is pierced with a knife.

5 ▲ Remove the chicken pieces from the pan and strain the cooking liquid. Discard the herbs, transfer the solids to a food processor and purée until smooth. Remove any fat from the cooking liquid and return to the casserole. Stir in the garlic and onion purée, return the chicken to the casserole and reheat gently for 3–4 minutes before serving.

# CHICKEN CHASSEUR

## *Poulet Sauté Chasseur*

*A chicken sauté is one of the classics of French cooking. Quick to prepare, it lends itself to endless variation. Since this dish reheats successfully, it is also convenient for entertaining.*

SERVES 4

*40g/1½oz/¼ cup plain (all-purpose) flour*
*1.2kg/2½lb chicken pieces*
*15ml/1 tbsp olive oil*
*3 small onions or large shallots, sliced*
*175g/6oz mushrooms, quartered*
*1 garlic clove, crushed*
*60ml/4 tbsp dry white wine*
*125ml/4fl oz/½ cup chicken stock*
*340g/¾lb tomatoes, peeled, seeded and chopped, or 250ml/8fl oz/1 cup canned chopped tomatoes*
*salt and freshly ground black pepper*
*fresh parsley, to garnish*

1 ▲ Put the flour into a polythene bag and season with salt and pepper. One at a time, drop the chicken pieces into the bag and shake to coat with flour. Tap off the excess and transfer to a plate.

2 ▲ Heat the oil in a heavy flameproof casserole. Fry the chicken over a medium-high heat until golden brown, turning once. Transfer to a plate and keep warm.

3 ▲ Pour off all but 15ml/1 tbsp of fat from the pan. Add the onions or shallots, mushrooms and garlic. Cook until golden, stirring frequently.

COOK'S TIP

To prepare ahead, reduce the cooking time by 5 minutes. Leave to cool and chill. Reheat gently for 15–20 minutes.

4 ▼ Return the chicken to the casserole with any juices. Add the wine and bring to the boil, then stir in the stock and tomatoes. Bring back to the boil, reduce the heat, cover and simmer over a low heat for about 20 minutes until the chicken is tender and the juices run clear when the thickest part of the meat is pierced with a knife. Tilt the pan and skim off any fat that has risen to the surface, then adjust the seasoning before serving.

# OLD-FASHIONED CHICKEN FRICASSÉE *Fricassée de Poulet*

*A* fricassée *is a classic dish in which poultry or meat is first seared in fat, then braised with liquid until cooked. This recipe is finished with a little cream – leave it out if you wish.*

SERVES 4–6

*1.2–1.3kg/$2\frac{1}{2}$–3lb chicken, cut into pieces*
*55g/2oz/4 tbsp butter*
*30ml/2 tbsp vegetable oil*
*30g/1oz/3 tbsp plain (all-purpose) flour*
*250ml/8fl oz/1 cup dry white wine*
*750ml/$1\frac{1}{4}$ pints/3 cups chicken stock*
*bouquet garni*
*1.5ml/$\frac{1}{4}$ tsp white pepper*
*225g/8oz button (white) mushrooms, trimmed*
*5ml/1 tsp lemon juice*
*16–24 small white onions, peeled*
*125ml/4fl oz/$\frac{1}{2}$ cup water*
*5ml/1 tsp sugar*
*90ml/6 tbsp whipping cream*
*salt*
*30ml/2 tbsp chopped fresh parsley, to garnish*

1 ▲ Wash the chicken pieces, then pat dry with kitchen paper. Melt half the butter with the oil in a large, heavy flameproof casserole over a medium heat. Add half the chicken pieces and cook for 10 minutes, turning occasionally, or until just golden in colour. Transfer to a plate, then cook the remaining pieces in the same way.

**COOK'S TIP**

This dish can be made ahead and kept hot in a warm oven for up to an hour before serving.

2 ▲ Return the seared chicken pieces to the casserole. Sprinkle with the flour, turning the pieces to coat. Cook over a low heat for about 4 minutes, turning occasionally.

3 ▲ Pour in the wine, bring to the boil and add the stock. Push the chicken pieces to one side and scrape the base of the casserole, stirring until well blended.

4 ▲ Bring the liquid to the boil, add the bouquet garni and season with a pinch of salt and white pepper. Cover and simmer over a medium heat for 25–30 minutes until the chicken is tender and the juices run clear when the thickest part of the meat is pierced with a knife.

5 ▲ Meanwhile, in a frying pan, heat the remaining butter over a medium-high heat. Add the mushrooms and lemon juice and cook for 3–4 minutes until the mushrooms are golden, stirring. Transfer the mushrooms to a bowl, add the onions, water and sugar to the pan, swirling to dissolve the sugar. Simmer for about 10 minutes, until just tender. Tip the onions and any juices into the bowl with the mushrooms and set aside.

6 When the chicken is cooked, transfer the pieces to a deep serving dish and cover with foil to keep warm. Discard the bouquet garni. Add any cooking juices from the vegetables to the casserole. Bring to the boil and boil, stirring frequently, until the sauce is reduced by half.

7 ▲ Whisk the cream into the sauce and cook for 2 minutes. Add the mushrooms and onions and cook for a further 2 minutes. Adjust the seasoning, then pour the sauce over the chicken, sprinkle with parsley and serve.

# Casseroled Rabbit with Thyme *Fricassée de Lapin au Thym*

*This is the sort of satisfying home cooking found in farmhouse kitchens and cosy neighbourhood restaurants in France, where rabbit is treated much like chicken and enjoyed frequently.*

Serves 4

*1.2kg/2½lb rabbit*
*40g/1½oz/¼ cup plain (all-purpose) flour*
*15g/½oz/1 tbsp butter*
*15ml/1 tbsp olive oil*
*250ml/8fl oz/1 cup red wine*
*350–500ml/12–16fl oz/1½–2 cups chicken stock*
*15ml/1 tbsp fresh thyme leaves, or 10ml/2 tsp dried thyme*
*1 bay leaf*
*2 garlic cloves, finely chopped*
*10–15ml/2–3 tsp Dijon mustard*
*salt and freshly ground black pepper*

1 Cut the rabbit into eight serving pieces: chop the saddle in half and separate the back legs into two pieces each; leave the front legs whole.

2 ▼ Put the flour in a polythene bag and season with salt and pepper. One at a time, drop the rabbit pieces into the bag and shake to coat them with flour. Tap off the excess, then discard any remaining flour.

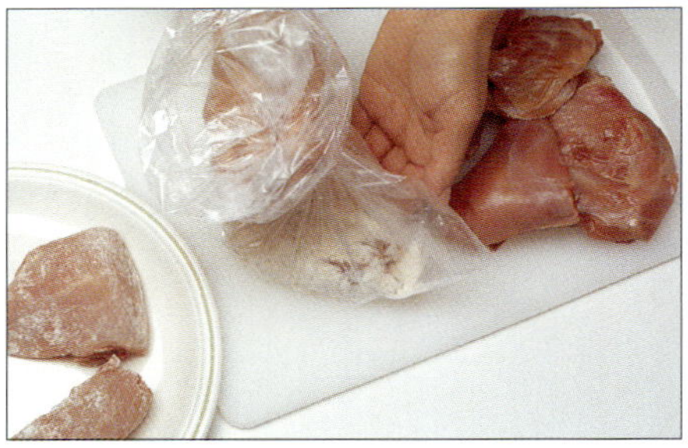

3 ▲ Melt the butter with the oil over a medium-high heat in a large flameproof casserole. Add the rabbit pieces and cook until golden, turning to colour evenly.

4 ▲ Add the wine and boil for 1 minute then add enough of the stock just to cover the meat. Add the herbs and garlic, then simmer gently, covered, for 1 hour, or until the rabbit is very tender and the juices run clear when the thickest part of the meat is pierced with a knife.

5 ▲ Stir in the mustard, adjust the seasoning and strain the sauce. Arrange the rabbit pieces on a warmed serving platter with some sauce and serve the rest separately.

# Guinea Fowl with Cabbage *Pintade au Chou*

*Guinea fowl is a domesticated relative of pheasant, so you can substitute pheasant or even chicken in this recipe. In some parts of France, such as Burgundy, garlic sausage may be added.*

Serves 4

*1.2–1.3kg/2½–3lb guinea fowl*
*15ml/1 tbsp vegetable oil*
*15g/½oz/1 tbsp butter*
*1 large onion, halved and sliced*
*1 large carrot, halved and sliced*
*1 large leek, sliced*
*450g/1lb green cabbage, such as savoy, sliced or chopped*
*125ml/4fl oz/½ cup dry white wine*
*125ml/4fl oz/½ cup chicken stock*
*1 or 2 garlic cloves, finely chopped*
*salt and freshly ground black pepper*

1 Preheat the oven to 180°C/350°F/Gas 4. Tie the legs of the guinea fowl with string.

2 ▲ Heat half the oil in a large flameproof casserole over a medium-high heat and cook the guinea fowl until golden brown on all sides. Transfer to a plate.

3 Pour out the fat from the casserole and add the remaining oil with the butter. Add the onion, carrot and leek and cook over a low heat, stirring occasionally, for 5 minutes. Add the cabbage and cook for about 3–4 minutes until slightly wilted, stirring occasionally. Season the vegetables with salt and pepper.

4 ▼ Place the guinea fowl on its side on the vegetables. Add the wine and bring to the boil, then add the stock and garlic. Cover and transfer to the oven. Cook for 25 minutes, then turn the bird on to the other side and cook for 20–25 minutes until it is tender and the juices run clear when the thickest part of the thigh is pierced with a knife.

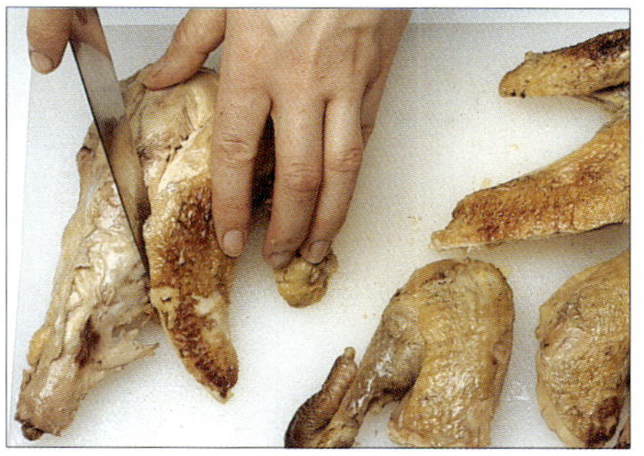

5 ▲ Transfer the bird to a board and leave to stand for 5–10 minutes, then cut into four or eight pieces. With a slotted spoon, transfer the cabbage to a warmed serving dish and place the guinea fowl on top. Skim any fat from the cooking juices and serve separately.

# ROAST PHEASANT WITH PORT *Faisan Rôti au Porto*

*Roasting the pheasant in foil keeps the flesh particularly moist. This recipe is best for very young birds and, if you have a choice, request the more tender female birds.*

SERVES 4

*2 oven-ready hen pheasants (about 675g/1½lb each)*
*55g/2oz/4 tbsp unsalted (sweet) butter, softened*
*8 fresh thyme sprigs*
*2 bay leaves*
*6 streaky (fatty) bacon rashers (strips)*
*15ml/1 tbsp plain (all-purpose) flour*
*175ml/6fl oz/¾ cup game or chicken stock, plus more if needed*
*15ml/1 tbsp redcurrant jelly*
*45–60ml/3–4 tbsp port*
*freshly ground black pepper*

1 Preheat the oven to 230°C/450°F/Gas 8. Line a large roasting pan with a sheet of strong foil large enough to enclose the pheasants. Lightly brush the foil with oil.

2 ▼ Wipe the pheasants with damp kitchen paper and remove any extra fat or skin. Using your fingertips, carefully loosen the skin of the breasts. With a round-bladed knife or small palette knife, spread the butter between the skin and breast meat of each bird. Tie the legs securely with string then lay the thyme sprigs and a bay leaf over the breast of each bird.

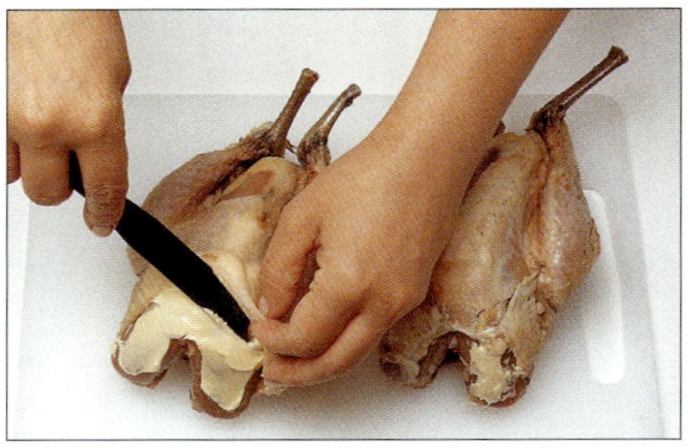

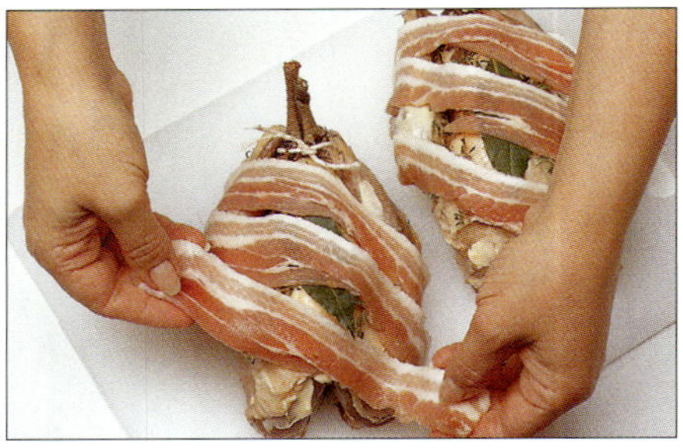

3 ▲ Lay bacon rashers over the breasts, place the birds in the foil-lined pan and season with pepper. Bring together the long ends of the foil, fold over securely to enclose, then seal the ends.

4 Roast the birds for 20 minutes, then reduce the oven temperature to 190°C/375°F/Gas 5 and cook for a further 40 minutes. Uncover the birds and roast 10–15 minutes more or until they are browned and the juices run clear when the thigh of a bird is pierced with a knife. Transfer the birds to a board and leave to stand, covered with clean foil, for 10 minutes before carving.

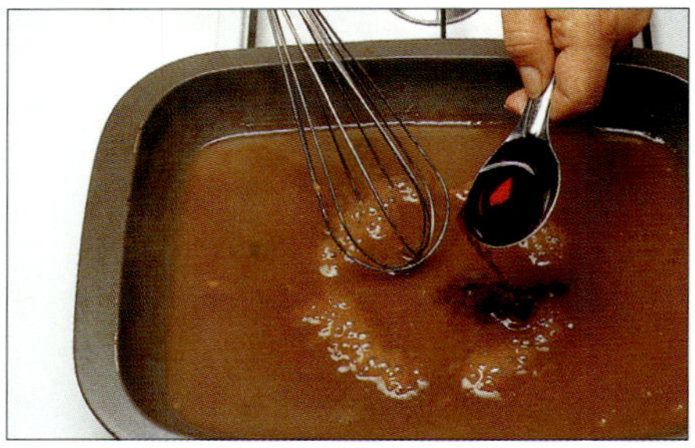

5 ▲ Pour the juices from the foil into the roasting pan and skim off any fat. Sprinkle in the flour and cook over a medium heat, stirring until smooth. Whisk in the stock and redcurrant jelly and bring to the boil. Simmer until the sauce thickens slightly, adding more stock if needed, then stir in the port and adjust the seasoning. Strain the sauce and serve with the pheasant.

# DUCK STEW WITH OLIVES *Ragoût de Canard aux Olives*

*This method of preparing duck has its roots in Provence. The sweetness of the onions, which are not typical in all regional versions, balances the saltiness of the olives.*

SERVES 6–8

*2 ducks (about 1.4kg/3¼lb each), quartered, or 8 duck leg quarters*
*225g/½lb baby onions*
*30ml/2 tbsp plain (all-purpose) flour*
*350ml/12fl oz/1½ cups dry red wine*
*500ml/16fl oz/2 cups duck or chicken stock*
*bouquet garni*
*100g/3½oz/1 cup stoned green or black olives, or a combination*
*salt, if needed, and freshly ground black pepper*

1 Put the duck pieces, skin side down, in a large frying pan over a medium heat and cook for 10–12 minutes until well browned, turning to colour evenly and cooking in batches if necessary. Pour off the fat from the pan.

2 Heat 15ml/1 tbsp of the duck fat in a large flameproof casserole and cook the onions, covered, over a medium-low heat until evenly browned, stirring frequently. Sprinkle with flour and continue cooking, uncovered, for 2 minutes, stirring frequently.

3 ▲ Stir in the wine and bring to the boil, then add the duck pieces, stock and bouquet garni. Bring to the boil, then reduce the heat to very low and simmer, covered, for about 40 minutes, stirring occasionally.

4 ▼ Rinse the olives in several changes of cold water. If they are very salty, put in a pan, cover with water and bring to the boil, then drain and rinse. Add the olives to the casserole and continue cooking for a further 20 minutes until the duck is very tender.

5 Transfer the duck pieces, onions and olives to a plate. Strain the cooking liquid, skim off all the fat and return the liquid to the pan. Boil to reduce by about one-third, then adjust the seasoning and return the duck and vegetables to the casserole. Simmer gently for a few minutes to heat through.

COOK'S TIP

If you take the breasts from whole ducks for duck breast recipes, freeze the legs until you have enough for this stew, and make stock from the carcasses.

It was in the year 1760 that a superior of the ancient religious order of Meaux transmitted to the Pommery family the « secret » « recipe » of their marvelous speciality

# MEAT DISHES

Meat is a mainstay of French country cooking. A pot of stew simmering on the back of the stove fills the farmhouse kitchen with enticing aromas and makes life easy for the cook. The pig from the neighbouring farm produces ham, sausages and succulent pork throughout the year. Sometimes these meats are combined with beans, lentils or sauerkraut for a hearty and warming treat. And what would Sunday lunch be without a roast – perhaps lamb served with vegetables from the garden. Every region has its traditional specialities for savoury meat dishes, and even in coastal areas the main course of the rural midday meal is likely to be meat.

# BURGUNDY BEEF STEW *Boeuf Bourguignon*

*Tradition dictates that you should use the same wine in this stew that you plan to serve with it, but a less expensive full-bodied wine will do for cooking. The stew reheats very well.*

SERVES 6

*1.5kg/3½lb lean stewing beef (chuck or shin)*
*175g/6oz lean salt pork or thick-cut rindless streaky (fatty) bacon*
*40g/1½oz/3 tbsp butter*
*350g/12oz baby onions*
*350g/12oz small button (white) mushrooms*
*1 onion, finely chopped*
*1 carrot, finely chopped*
*2 or 3 garlic cloves, finely chopped*
*45ml/3 tbsp plain (all-purpose) flour*
*750ml/1¼ pints/3 cups red wine, preferably Burgundy*
*25ml/1½ tbsp tomato purée (paste)*
*bouquet garni*
*600–750ml/1–1¼ pints/2½-3 cups beef stock*
*15ml/1 tbsp chopped fresh parsley*
*salt and freshly ground black pepper*

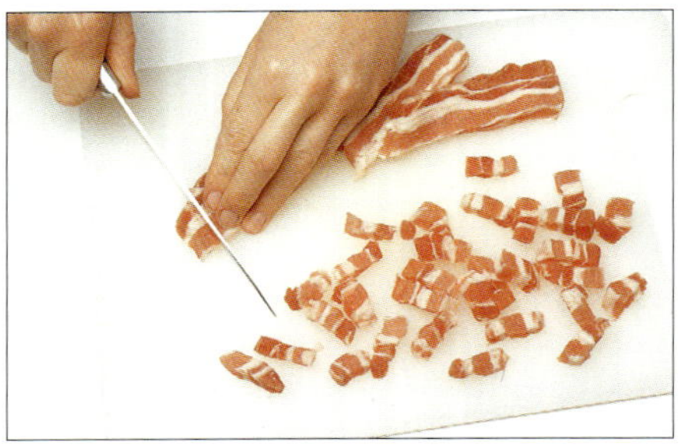

1 ▲ Cut the beef into 5cm/2in pieces and dice the salt pork or cut the bacon crossways into thin strips.

2 In a large heavy flameproof casserole, cook the pork or bacon over a medium heat until golden brown, then remove with a slotted spoon and drain. Pour off all but 30ml/2 tbsp of the fat.

3 ▲ Increase the heat to medium-high. Add enough meat to the pan to fit easily in one layer (do not crowd the pan or the meat will not brown) and cook, turning to colour all sides, until well browned. Transfer the beef to a plate and continue browning the meat in batches.

4 ▲ In a heavy frying pan, melt one-third of the butter over a medium heat, add the baby onions and cook, stirring frequently, until evenly golden. Set aside on a plate.

5 ▲ In the same pan, melt half of the remaining butter over a medium heat. Add the mushrooms and sauté, stirring frequently, until golden, then set aside with the baby onions.

6 ▲ When all the beef has been browned, pour off any fat from the casserole and add the remaining butter. When the butter has melted, add the onion, carrot and garlic and cook over a medium heat for about 3–4 minutes until just softened, stirring frequently. Sprinkle over the flour and cook for 2 minutes, then add the wine, tomato purée and bouquet garni. Bring to the boil, scraping the base of the pan.

7 ▲ Return the beef and bacon to the casserole and pour on the stock, adding more if needed to cover the meat and vegetables when pressed down. Cover the casserole and simmer very gently over a low heat, stirring occasionally, for about 3 hours or until the meat is very tender. Add the sautéed mushrooms and baby onions and cook, covered, for a further 30 minutes. Discard the bouquet garni and stir in the parsley before serving.

Beaune

# STEAK WITH ANCHOVY SAUCE *Entrecôte au Beurre d'Anchois*

*This may sound like an unusual combination, but the anchovy adds flavour without tasting fishy.*

SERVES 2

*40g/1½oz/3 tbsp butter*
*4 shallots, finely chopped*
*1 garlic clove, crushed*
*100ml/3½fl oz/6 tbsp whipping cream*
*25ml/1½ tbsp anchovy paste*
*15ml/1 tbsp chopped fresh tarragon*
*2 sirloin or fillet steaks, about 200–250g/7–9oz each*
*10ml/2 tsp vegetable oil*
*salt and freshly ground black pepper*
*parsley or tarragon sprigs, to garnish*
*sautéed potatoes, to serve*

1 ▼ Melt 30g/1oz/2 tbsp of the butter in a small pan and fry the shallots and garlic until they are just soft. Stir in the cream, anchovy paste and tarragon, and simmer very gently for about 10 minutes.

2 ▲ Season the steaks. Heat the remaining butter with the oil in a heavy frying pan over a medium-high heat until it begins to brown.

3 Add the meat and cook for about 6–8 minutes, turning once, until done as preferred (medium-rare meat will still be slightly soft when pressed, medium meat will be springy and well-done firm.) Transfer the steaks to warmed serving plates and cover to keep warm.

4 ▲ Add 30ml/2 tbsp water to the frying pan. Stir in the anchovy sauce and cook for 1–2 minutes, stirring and scraping the bottom of the pan. Adjust the seasoning and pour the sauce over the meat, then garnish with parsley or tarragon and serve with potatoes.

VARIATION

To make a tomato cream sauce to serve with the steak, substitute 5–10ml/1–2 tsp tomato purée (paste) for the anchovy paste.

# VEAL KIDNEYS WITH MUSTARD *Rognons de Veau à la Moutarde*

*In France, veal kidneys are easily found, but this dish is equally delicious made with lamb's kidneys. Be sure not to cook the sauce too long once the mustard is added or it will lose its piquancy.*

SERVES 4

*2 veal kidneys or 8–10 lamb's kidneys, trimmed and membranes removed*
*30g/1oz/2 tbsp butter*
*15ml/1 tbsp vegetable oil*
*120g/4oz button (white) mushrooms, quartered*
*60ml/4 tbsp chicken stock*
*30ml/2 tbsp brandy (optional)*
*175ml/6fl oz/¾ cup crème fraîche or double (heavy) cream*
*30ml/2 tbsp Dijon mustard*
*salt and freshly ground black pepper*
*chopped fresh chives, to garnish*

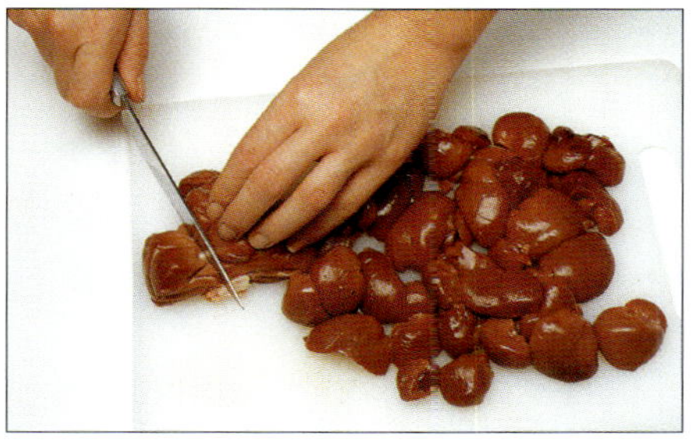

1 ▲ Cut the veal kidneys into pieces, discarding any fat. If using lamb's kidneys, remove the central core by cutting a V-shape from the middle of each kidney. Cut each kidney into three or four pieces.

2 ▲ In a large frying pan, melt the butter with the oil over a high heat and swirl to blend. Add the kidneys and sauté for about 3–4 minutes, stirring frequently, until well browned, then transfer them to a plate using a slotted spoon.

3 ▲ Add the mushrooms to the pan and sauté for 2–3 minutes until golden, stirring frequently. Pour in the chicken stock and brandy, if using, then bring to the boil and boil for 2 minutes.

4 ▼ Stir in the crème fraîche or double cream and cook for about 2–3 minutes until the sauce has slightly thickened. Stir in the mustard and season, then add the kidneys and cook for 1 minute to reheat. Sprinkle over the chives before serving.

# ROAST STUFFED LAMB *Gigot Farcie*

*The lambs which graze in the salty marshes along the north coast of Brittany and Normandy are considered the best in France. The stuffing is suitable for either leg or shoulder joints.*

SERVES 6–8

*1.8–2kg/4–4½lb boneless leg or shoulder of lamb (not tied)*
*30g/1oz/2 tbsp butter, softened*
*15–30ml/1–2 tbsp plain (all-purpose) flour*
*125ml/4fl oz/½ cup white wine*
*250ml/8fl oz/1 cup chicken or beef stock*
*salt and freshly ground black pepper*
*watercress, to garnish*
*sautéed potatoes, to serve*

FOR THE STUFFING
*70g/2½oz/5 tbsp butter*
*1 small onion, finely chopped*
*1 garlic clove, finely chopped*
*55g/2oz/⅓ cup long grain rice*
*150ml/¼ pint/⅔ cup chicken stock*
*2.5ml/½ tsp dried thyme*
*4 lamb's kidneys, halved and cored*
*275g/10oz young spinach leaves, well washed*
*salt and freshly ground black pepper*

1 ▲ To make the stuffing, melt 30g/1oz/2 tbsp of the butter in a pan over a medium heat. Add the onion and cook for 2–3 minutes until just softened, then add the garlic and rice and cook for about 1–2 minutes until the rice appears translucent, stirring constantly. Add the stock, salt and pepper and thyme and bring to the boil, stirring occasionally, then reduce the heat to low and cook for about 18 minutes, covered, until the rice is tender and the liquid is absorbed. Tip the rice into a bowl and fluff with a fork.

2 In a small frying pan, melt about 30g/1oz/2 tbsp of the remaining butter over a medium-high heat. Add the kidneys and cook for about 2–3 minutes, turning once, until lightly browned, but still pink inside, then transfer to a board and leave to cool. Cut the kidneys into pieces and add to the rice, season with salt and pepper and toss to combine.

3 In a frying pan, heat the remaining butter over a medium heat until foaming. Add the spinach leaves and cook for 1–2 minutes until wilted, drain off excess liquid, then transfer the leaves to a plate and leave to cool.

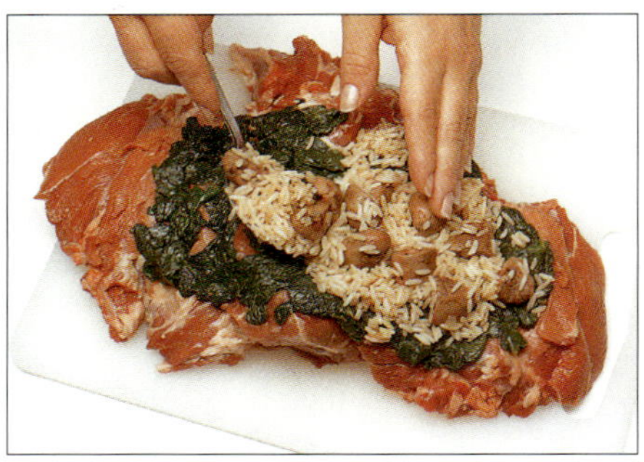

4 ▲ Preheat the oven to 190°C/375°F/Gas 5. Lay the meat skin side down on a work surface and season with salt and pepper. Spread the spinach leaves in an even layer over the surface then spread the stuffing in an even layer over the spinach. Roll up the meat like a Swiss roll and use a skewer to close the seam.

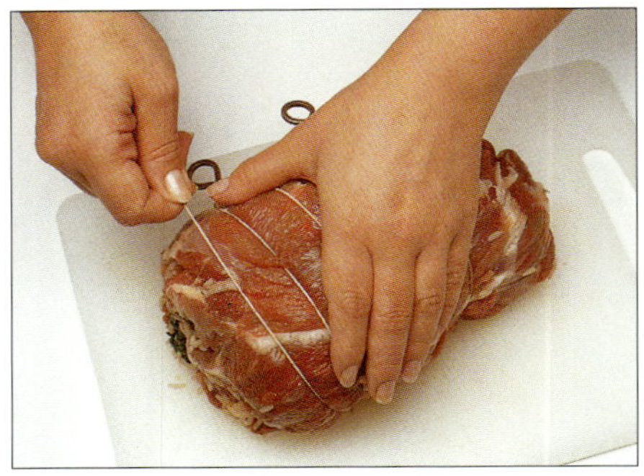

5 ▲ Tie the meat at 2.5cm/1 in intervals to hold its shape, then place in a roasting pan, spread with the softened butter and season with salt and pepper. Roast for 1½–2 hours until the juices run slightly pink when pierced with a skewer, or until a meat thermometer inserted into the thickest part of the meat registers 57–60°C/135–140°F (for medium-rare to medium). Transfer the meat to a carving board, cover loosely with foil and leave to rest for about 20 minutes.

6 Skim off as much fat from the roasting pan as possible, then place the pan over a medium-high heat and bring to the boil. Sprinkle over the flour and cook for 2–3 minutes until browned, stirring and scraping the base of the pan. Whisk in the wine and stock and bring to the boil, then cook for 4–5 minutes until the sauce thickens. Season and strain into a gravy boat. Carve the meat into slices, garnish with watercress and serve with the gravy and potatoes.

VARIATION

If kidneys are difficult to obtain, substitute about 125g/¼lb mushrooms. Chop them coarsely and cook in the butter until tender. Don't use dark mushrooms – they will make the rice a murky colour.

# SAUERKRAUT WITH PORK AND SAUSAGES *Choucroûte Garnie*

*This Alsatian speciality shows the German influence on the region's cuisine. Strasbourg is renowned for its pork and beef sausages – use them if you can.*

SERVES 8

*30ml/2 tbsp vegetable oil*
*1 onion, halved and sliced*
*120g/4oz smoked rindless streaky (fatty) bacon rashers (strips), chopped*
*900g/2lb bottled sauerkraut, well rinsed and drained*
*1 apple, peeled and sliced*
*1 or 2 bay leaves*
*2.5ml/½ tsp dried thyme*
*4–5 juniper berries*
*250ml/8fl oz/1 cup dry white wine*
*125ml/4fl oz/½ cup apple juice or water*
*6 Strasbourg sausages, knackwurst or frankfurters*
*6 spare ribs*
*900g/2lb small potatoes, peeled*
*4 smoked gammon (smoked or cured ham) chops or steaks*

1 ▼ Preheat the oven to 150°C/300°F/Gas 2. Heat half the oil in a large flameproof casserole over a medium heat, then add the onion and bacon and cook, stirring occasionally for about 5 minutes until the onion is soft and the bacon just coloured.

2 ▲ Tilt the pan and spoon off as much fat as possible, then stir in the sauerkraut, apple, bay leaves, thyme, juniper, wine and apple juice or water. Cover the casserole, place in the oven and cook for 30 minutes.

3 In a second large flameproof casserole, heat the remaining oil over a medium-high heat and add the spare ribs. Cook, turning frequently, until browned on all sides. Add the spare ribs to the other casserole with the sausages and cook, covered, for 1½ hours, stirring occasionally.

4 ▲ Bring a large pan of lightly salted water to the boil over a medium-high heat. Add the potatoes, cook for 10 minutes, drain and add to the casserole with the pork chops. Push them into the sauerkraut and continue cooking, covered, for 30–45 minutes more. Season with salt, if needed, and pepper before serving.

# TOULOUSE CASSOULET *Cassoulet*

*There are as many versions of this regional speciality in South-west France as there are towns.*

SERVES 6–8

*450g/1lb dried haricot (navy) or cannellini beans, soaked overnight in cold water, then rinsed and drained*
*675g/1½lb Toulouse sausages*
*550g/1¼lb each boneless lamb and pork shoulder, cut into 5cm/2in pieces*
*1 large onion, finely chopped*
*3 or 4 garlic cloves, very finely chopped*
*4 tomatoes, peeled, seeded and chopped*
*300ml/½ pint/1¼ cups chicken stock*
*bouquet garni*
*60ml/4 tbsp fresh breadcrumbs*
*salt and freshly ground black pepper*

1 Put the beans in a pan with water to cover. Boil vigorously for 10 minutes and drain, then return to a clean pan, cover with water and bring to the boil. Reduce the heat and simmer for 45 minutes, or until tender, then add a little salt and leave to soak in the cooking water.

2 ▲ Preheat the oven to 180°C/350°F/Gas 4. Prick the sausages, place them in a large heavy frying pan over a medium heat and cook for 20–25 minutes until browned, turning occasionally. Drain on kitchen paper and pour off all but 15ml/1 tbsp of the fat from the pan.

3 Increase the heat to medium-high. Season the lamb and pork and add enough of the meat to the pan to fit easily in one layer. Cook until browned, then transfer to a large dish. Continue browning in batches.

4 Add the onion and garlic to the pan and cook for 3–4 minutes until just soft, stirring. Stir in the tomatoes and cook for 2–3 minutes, then transfer the vegetables to the meat dish. Add the stock and bring to the boil, then skim off the fat.

5 ▲ Spoon a quarter of the beans into a large casserole, and top with a third of the sausages, meat and vegetables.

6 Continue layering, ending with a layer of beans. Tuck in the bouquet garni, pour over the stock and top up with enough of the bean cooking liquid to just cover.

7 Cover the casserole and bake for 2 hours (check and add more bean cooking liquid if it seems dry). Uncover the casserole, sprinkle over the breadcrumbs and press with the back of a spoon to moisten them. Continue cooking the cassoulet, uncovered, for about 20 minutes more until browned.

# COUNTRY-STYLE PÂTÉ WITH LEEKS *Pâté de Porc aux Poireaux*

*Traditionally this sort of pork pâté (or more correctly, terrine, since it has no crust) contains pork liver and egg to bind. This version uses leeks instead for a fresher flavour and a lighter result.*

SERVES 8–10

*450g/1lb trimmed leeks (white and light green parts)*
*15g/½oz/1 tbsp butter*
*2 or 3 large garlic cloves, finely chopped*
*1kg/2¼lb lean pork leg or shoulder*
*150g/5oz smoked rindless streaky (fatty) bacon rashers (strips)*
*7.5ml/1½ tsp chopped fresh thyme*
*3 sage leaves, finely chopped*
*1.5ml/¼ tsp* quatre èpices *(a mix of ground cloves, cinnamon, nutmeg and pepper)*
*1.5ml/¼ tsp ground cumin*
*pinch of freshly grated nutmeg*
*2.5ml/½ tsp salt*
*5ml/1 tsp freshly ground black pepper*
*1 bay leaf*

1 ▲ Cut the leeks lengthways, wash well and slice thinly. Melt the butter in a large heavy pan, add the leeks, then cover and cook over a medium-low heat for 10 minutes, stirring occasionally. Add the garlic and continue cooking for about 10 minutes until the leeks are very soft, then set aside to cool.

COOK'S TIP

In France, *cornichons* (small dill pickles) and mustard are traditional accompaniments for pork terrines along with slices of crusty baguette.

2 ▲ Trim all the fat, tendons and connective tissue from the pork and cut the meat into 3.5cm/1¾in cubes. Working in two or three batches, put the meat into a food processor fitted with the metal blade; the bowl should be about half-full. Pulse to chop the meat to a coarse purée. Alternatively, pass the meat through the coarse blade of a meat mincer. Transfer the meat to a large mixing bowl and remove any white stringy bits.

3 Reserve two of the bacon rashers for garnishing, and chop or grind the remainder. Add the bacon to the pork in the bowl.

4 Preheat the oven to 180°C/350°F/Gas 4. Line the base and sides of a 1.5 litre/2½ pint/6¼ cup terrine or loaf tin (pan) with baking parchment.

5 ▲ Add the leeks, herbs, spices and salt and pepper to the bowl with the pork and bacon and, using a wooden spoon or your fingertips, mix until well combined.

6 ▲ Spoon the mixture into the terrine or loaf tin, pressing it into the corners and compacting it. Tap firmly to settle the mixture and smooth the top. Arrange the bay leaf and bacon rashers on top, then cover tightly with foil.

7 ▲ Place the terrine or loaf tin in a roasting tin and pour boiling water to come halfway up the sides. Bake for 1¼ hours.

8 Lift the terrine or tin out of the roasting tin and pour out the water. Put the terrine back in the roasting tin and place a baking sheet or board on top. If the pâté has not risen above the sides of the terrine, place a foil-covered board directly on the pâté. Weight with two or three large cans or other heavy objects while it cools. (Liquid will seep out which is why the terrine should stand inside a roasting tin.) Chill until cold, preferably overnight, before slicing.

Mustard Pommery
HUIC CONDIMENTO EST IMPERARE OMNIBUS CIBIS
A.D. 1632
OUTARDE DE MEAUX
POMMERY
AROMATISÉE

# PASTRY AND CAKES

Home baking is a recent development in rural areas of France, where the communal bread oven was used for baking cakes and tarts in the heat remaining from the weekly batch of bread. Now *pâtisseries* appear in practically every town and a country market usually has a stall of regional sweet treats, such as the traditional butter biscuits (cookies) of Brittany. Elaborate pastries and cakes are normally the province of professionals, but country cooks are more likely than their urban counterparts to make tea cakes and fruit tarts themselves – apple tarts are a great way to use windfall apples from the orchard – and most have a treasured recipe for a rich, homely chocolate cake.

# POUND CAKE WITH RED FRUIT *Quatre Quarts aux Fruits*

Quatre quarts *literally translates as "four quarters", in this case, the equal amounts of the four main ingredients. This orange-scented cake is good with tea or as a dessert with a fruit* coulis.

SERVES 6–8

*450g/1lb fresh raspberries, strawberries or stoned (pitted) cherries, or a combination of any of these*
*175g/6oz/⅞ cup caster (superfine) sugar, plus 15–30ml/1–2 tbsp and extra for sprinkling*
*15ml/1 tbsp lemon juice*
*175g/6oz/1⅓ cup plain (all-purpose) flour*
*10ml/2 tsp baking powder*
*pinch of salt*
*175g/6oz/¾ cup unsalted (sweet) butter, softened*
*3 eggs, at room temperature*
*grated rind of 1 orange*
*15ml/1 tbsp orange juice*

1 Reserve a few whole fruits for decorating. In a food processor fitted with the metal blade, process the fruit until smooth.

2 ▼ Add 15–30ml/1–2 tbsp of the sugar and the lemon juice to the fruit purée, then process again to blend. Strain the sauce and chill.

3 Butter the base and sides of a 20×10cm/8×4in loaf tin (pan) or a 20cm/ 8in springform tin (pan) and line the base with baking parchment. Butter the paper and the sides of the tin again, then sprinkle lightly with sugar and tip out any excess. Preheat the oven to 180°C/350°F/Gas 4.

4 ▲ Sift the flour, baking powder and a pinch of salt. In a medium bowl, beat the butter with an electric mixer for 1 minute until creamy. Add the sugar and beat for 4–5 minutes until very light and fluffy, then add the eggs, one at a time, beating well after each addition. Beat in the orange rind and juice.

5 ▲ Gently fold the flour mixture into the butter mixture in three batches, then spoon the mixture into the prepared tin and tap gently to release any air bubbles.

6 Bake the cake for 35–40 minutes until the top is golden and springs back when touched. Transfer the cake in its tin to a wire rack and leave to cool for 10 minutes. Remove the cake from the tin, then cool for about ½ hour. Remove the paper and serve slices or wedges of the warm cake with a little of the fruit sauce and decorate with the reserved fruit.

# Individual Brioches *Petites Brioches*

*These buttery rolls with their distinctive little topknots are delicious with a spoonful or two of jam and a cup of* café au lait *– or try them split and filled with scrambled eggs.*

Makes 8

*7g/¼oz/scant 1 tbsp active dry yeast*
*15ml/1 tbsp caster (superfine) sugar*
*30ml/2 tbsp warm milk*
*2 eggs*
*about 200g/7oz/1½ cups plain (all-purpose) flour*
*2.5ml/½ tsp salt*
*85g/3oz/6 tbsp butter, cut into 6 pieces, at room temperature*
*1 egg yolk beaten with 10ml/2 tsp water, for glazing*

1 ▲ Lightly butter eight individual brioche or muffin tins (pans). Put the yeast and sugar in a small bowl, add the milk and stir until dissolved. Leave to stand for about 5 minutes until foamy, then beat in the egg.

2 ▲ Put the flour and salt into a food processor fitted with the metal blade, then with the machine running, slowly pour in the yeast mixture. Scrape down the sides and continue processing for about 2–3 minutes, or until the dough forms a ball. Add the butter and pulse about 10 times, or until the butter is incorporated.

3 Transfer the dough to a lightly buttered bowl and cover with a cloth. Set aside to rise in a warm place for about 1 hour until doubled in size, then punch down.

4 ▲ Set aside one-quarter of the dough. Shape the remaining dough into eight balls and put into the prepared tins. Shape the reserved dough into eight smaller balls, then make a depression in the top of each large ball and set a small ball into it.

5 Allow the brioches to rise in a warm place for about 30 minutes until doubled in size. Preheat the oven to 200°C/400°F/Gas 6.

6 Brush the brioches lightly with the egg glaze and bake them for 15–18 minutes until golden brown. Transfer to a wire rack and leave to cool before serving.

Cook's tip

The dough may also be baked in the characteristic large brioche tin (pan) with sloping fluted sides. Put about three-quarters of the dough into the tin and set the remainder in a depression in the top, cover and leave to rise for about 1 hour, then bake for 35–45 minutes.

# LEMON TART *Tarte au Citron*

*This tart has a refreshing tangy flavour. You can find it in bistros and* pâtisseries *all over France.*

SERVES 8–10

*340g/12oz shortcrust pastry*
*grated rind of 2 or 3 lemons*
*150ml/¼ pint/⅔ cup freshly squeezed lemon juice*
*100g/3½oz/½ cup caster (superfine) sugar*
*60ml/4 tbsp crème fraîche or double (heavy) cream*
*4 eggs, plus 3 egg yolks*
*icing (confectioners') sugar, for dusting*

1 ▼ Preheat the oven to 190°C/375°F/Gas 5. Roll out the pastry thinly and use to line a 23cm/9in flan tin (tart pan). Prick the base.

2 ▲ Line the pastry case with foil and fill with baking beans. Bake for about 15 minutes until the edges are set and dry. Remove the foil and beans and continue baking for a further 5–7 minutes until golden.

3 ▲ Place the lemon rind, juice and sugar in a bowl. Beat until combined and then gradually add the crème fraîche or double cream and beat until well blended.

4 ▲ Beat in the eggs, one at a time, then beat in the egg yolks and pour the filling into the pastry case. Bake for 15–20 minutes, until the filling is set. If the pastry begins to brown too much, cover the edges with foil. Leave to cool. Dust with icing sugar before serving.

# INDIVIDUAL BRIOCHES

## *Petites Brioches*

*These buttery rolls with their distinctive little topknots are delicious with a spoonful or two of jam and a cup of* café au lait *– or try them split and filled with scrambled eggs.*

### MAKES 8

*7g/¼oz/scant 1 tbsp active dry yeast*
*15ml/1 tbsp caster (superfine) sugar*
*30ml/2 tbsp warm milk*
*2 eggs*
*about 200g/7oz/1½ cups plain (all-purpose) flour*
*2.5ml/½ tsp salt*
*85g/3oz/6 tbsp butter, cut into 6 pieces, at room temperature*
*1 egg yolk beaten with 10ml/2 tsp water, for glazing*

1 ▲ Lightly butter eight individual brioche or muffin tins (pans). Put the yeast and sugar in a small bowl, add the milk and stir until dissolved. Leave to stand for about 5 minutes until foamy, then beat in the egg.

2 ▲ Put the flour and salt into a food processor fitted with the metal blade, then with the machine running, slowly pour in the yeast mixture. Scrape down the sides and continue processing for about 2–3 minutes, or until the dough forms a ball. Add the butter and pulse about 10 times, or until the butter is incorporated.

3 Transfer the dough to a lightly buttered bowl and cover with a cloth. Set aside to rise in a warm place for about 1 hour until doubled in size, then punch down.

4 ▲ Set aside one-quarter of the dough. Shape the remaining dough into eight balls and put into the prepared tins. Shape the reserved dough into eight smaller balls, then make a depression in the top of each large ball and set a small ball into it.

5 Allow the brioches to rise in a warm place for about 30 minutes until doubled in size. Preheat the oven to 200°C/400°F/Gas 6.

6 Brush the brioches lightly with the egg glaze and bake them for 15–18 minutes until golden brown. Transfer to a wire rack and leave to cool before serving.

### COOK'S TIP

The dough may also be baked in the characteristic large brioche tin (pan) with sloping fluted sides. Put about three-quarters of the dough into the tin and set the remainder in a depression in the top, cover and leave to rise for about 1 hour, then bake for 35–45 minutes.

# Brittany Butter Biscuits *Petites Gâteaux Bretons*

*These biscuits are similar to shortbread, but richer. Like most of the cakes and pastries from this province, they are made with the lightly salted butter,* beurre demi-sel, *from around Nantes.*

Makes 18–20

*6 egg yolks, lightly beaten*
*15ml/1 tbsp milk*
*250g/9oz/2 cups plain (all-purpose) flour*
*175g/6oz/⅞ cup caster (superfine) sugar*
*200g/7oz/⅞ cup lightly salted butter, at room temperature, cut into small pieces*

### Cook's tip

For one large Brittany Butter Cake, pat the dough with well-floured hands into a 23cm/9in loose-based cake tin (pan) or springform tin (pan). Brush with egg glaze and score the pattern on top. Bake for 45 minutes–1 hour until firm and golden brown.

1 Preheat the oven to 180°C/350°F/Gas 4. Lightly butter a large heavy baking sheet. Mix 15ml/1 tbsp of the egg yolks with the milk to make a glaze and set aside.

2 ▲ Sift the flour into a large bowl and make a well in the centre. Add the egg yolks, sugar and butter and, using your fingertips, work them together until smooth and creamy.

3 ▲ Gradually bring in a little flour at a time from the edge of the well, working it to form a smooth, slightly sticky dough.

4 ▲ Using floured hands, pat out the dough to about a 8mm/¾in thickness and cut out rounds using a 7.5cm/3in cutter. Transfer the rounds to a baking sheet, brush each with a little egg glaze, then using the back of a knife, score with lines to create a lattice pattern.

5 Bake the biscuits (cookies) for about 12–15 minutes until golden. Cool in the tin on a wire rack for 15 minutes, then carefully remove the biscuits and leave to cool completely on the rack. Store in an airtight container.

# SPICED-NUT PALMIERS *Palmiers*

*These delicate pastries, said to resemble palm trees, are popular throughout France. They are often simply rolled in sugar, but in this recipe the filling includes cinnamon and nuts.*

**MAKES ABOUT 40**

*75g/2¾oz/½ cup chopped almonds, walnuts or hazelnuts*
*30ml/2 tbsp caster (superfine) sugar, plus extra for sprinkling*
*2.5ml/½ tsp ground cinnamon*
*225g/½lb rough-puff or puff pastry, defrosted if frozen*
*1 egg, lightly beaten*

1 ▲ Lightly butter two large baking sheets, preferably non-stick. In a food processor fitted with a metal blade, process the nuts, sugar and cinnamon until finely ground. Transfer half to a small bowl.

2 ▲ Sprinkle the work surface and pastry with sugar and roll out the pastry to a 50×20cm/20×8in rectangle about 3mm/⅛in thick, sprinkling with more sugar as necessary. Brush the pastry lightly with beaten egg and sprinkle evenly with half of the nut mixture in the bowl.

3 ▼ Fold in the long edges of the pastry to meet in the centre and flatten with the rolling pin. Brush with egg and sprinkle with most of the nut mixture. Fold in the edges again to meet in the centre, brush with egg and sprinkle with the remaining nut mixture. Fold one side of the pastry over the other.

4 Using a sharp knife, cut the pastry crossways into 8mm/⅜in thick slices and place the pieces cut-side down about 2.5cm/1in apart on the baking sheets.

5 ▲ Spread the pastry edges apart to form a wedge shape. Chill the palmiers for at least 15 minutes. Preheat oven to 220°C/425°F/Gas 7.

6 Bake the palmiers for about 8–10 minutes until golden, carefully turning them over halfway through the cooking time. Watch carefully as the sugar can easily scorch. Transfer to a wire rack to cool.

# LEMON TART

*Tarte au Citron*

*This tart has a refreshing tangy flavour. You can find it in bistros and* pâtisseries *all over France.*

SERVES 8–10

*340g/12oz shortcrust pastry*
*grated rind of 2 or 3 lemons*
*150ml/¼ pint/⅔ cup freshly squeezed lemon juice*
*100g/3½oz/½ cup caster (superfine) sugar*
*60ml/4 tbsp crème fraîche or double (heavy) cream*
*4 eggs, plus 3 egg yolks*
*icing (confectioners') sugar, for dusting*

1 ▼ Preheat the oven to 190°C/375°F/Gas 5. Roll out the pastry thinly and use to line a 23cm/9in flan tin (tart pan). Prick the base.

2 ▲ Line the pastry case with foil and fill with baking beans. Bake for about 15 minutes until the edges are set and dry. Remove the foil and beans and continue baking for a further 5–7 minutes until golden.

3 ▲ Place the lemon rind, juice and sugar in a bowl. Beat until combined and then gradually add the crème fraîche or double cream and beat until well blended.

4 ▲ Beat in the eggs, one at a time, then beat in the egg yolks and pour the filling into the pastry case. Bake for 15–20 minutes, until the filling is set. If the pastry begins to brown too much, cover the edges with foil. Leave to cool. Dust with icing sugar before serving.

# FRENCH CHOCOLATE CAKE *Gâteau au Chocolat*

*This is typical of a French home-made cake – dense, dark and delicious. The texture is very different from a sponge cake and it is excellent served with cream or a fruit* coulis.

SERVES 10–12

*150g/5oz/¾ cup caster (superfine) sugar, plus extra for sprinkling*
*275g/10oz plain (semisweet) chocolate, chopped*
*175g/6oz/¾ cup unsalted (sweet) butter, cut into pieces*
*10ml/2 tsp vanilla essence (extract)*
*5 eggs, separated*
*40g/1½oz/¼ cup plain (all-purpose) flour, sifted*
*pinch of salt*
*icing (confectioners') sugar, for dusting*

1 ▲ Preheat the oven to 170°C/325°F/Gas 3. Generously butter a 24cm/9½in springform tin (pan), then sprinkle the tin with a little sugar and tap out the excess.

2 Set aside 45ml/3 tbsp of the sugar. Place the chocolate, butter and remaining sugar in a heavy pan and cook over a low heat until the chocolate and butter have melted and the sugar has dissolved. Remove the pan from the heat, stir in the vanilla essence and leave the mixture to cool slightly.

3 ▼ Beat the egg yolks into the chocolate mixture, beating each in well, then stir in the flour.

4 In a clean greasefree bowl, using an electric mixer, beat the egg whites slowly until they are frothy. Increase the speed, add the salt and continue beating until soft peaks form. Sprinkle over the reserved sugar and beat until the whites are stiff and glossy. Beat one third of the whites into the chocolate mixture, then fold in the remaining whites.

5 ▲ Carefully pour the mixture into the tin and tap the tin gently to release any air bubbles.

6 Bake the cake for about 35–45 minutes until well risen and the top springs back when touched lightly with a fingertip. (If the cake appears to rise unevenly, rotate after 20–25 minutes.) Transfer the cake to a wire rack, remove the sides of the tin and leave to cool completely. Remove the tin base. Dust the cake with icing sugar and transfer to a serving plate.

# APPLE TART

*Tarte aux Pommes*

*This easy-to-make apple tart has rustic charm – it is just as you might find in a French farmhouse. Cooking the apples before putting them on the pastry prevents a soggy crust.*

SERVES 6

*900g/2lb medium cooking apples, peeled, quartered and cored*
*15ml/1 tbsp lemon juice*
*55g/2oz/¼ cup caster (superfine) sugar*
*40g/1½oz/4 tbsp butter*
*350g/¾lb shortcrust or sweet pastry*
*crème fraîche or lightly whipped cream, to serve*

**VARIATION**

For Spiced Pear Tart, substitute pears for the apples, cooking them for about 10 minutes until golden. Sprinkle with 2.5ml/½ tsp ground cinnamon and a pinch of ground cloves and stir to combine before arranging on the pastry

1 Cut each cooking apple quarter lengthways into two or three slices. Sprinkle with lemon juice and sugar and toss to combine.

2 ▲ Melt the butter in a large heavy frying pan over a medium heat and add the apples. Cook, stirring frequently, for about 12 minutes until the apples are just golden brown. Remove the frying pan from the heat and set aside. Preheat the oven to 190°C/375°F/Gas 5.

3 ▲ On a lightly floured surface, roll out the pastry to a 30cm/12in round and trim the edge if uneven. Carefully transfer the pastry round to a baking sheet.

4 ▲ Spoon the apple slices on to the pastry round, heaping them up, and leaving a 5cm/2in border all round the edge of the pastry.

5 ▲ Turn up the pastry border and gather it around the apples to enclose the outside apples. Bake the tart for 35–40 minutes until the pastry is crisp and browned. Serve warm, with crème fraîche or cream.

# Pear and Almond Cream Tart *Tarte aux Poires Frangipane*

*This tart is equally successful made with other kinds of fruit, and some variation can be seen in almost every good French* pâtisserie. *Try making it with nectarines, peaches, apricots or apples.*

Serves 6

*3 firm pears*
*lemon juice*
*350g/¾lb shortcrust pastry*
*15ml/1 tbsp peach brandy or water*
*60ml/4 tbsp peach preserve, strained*
For the almond cream filling
*100g/3½oz/¾ cup blanched whole almonds*
*55g/2oz/¼ cup caster (superfine) sugar*
*70g/2½oz/5 tbsp butter*
*1 egg, plus 1 egg white*
*few drops almond essence (extract)*

1 ▲ Roll out the pastry thinly and use to line a 23cm/9in flan tin (tart pan). Chill the pastry case while you make the filling. Put the almonds and sugar in a food processor fitted with the metal blade and pulse until finely ground; they should not be pasty. Add the butter and process until creamy, then add the egg, egg white and almond essence and mix well.

2 Place a baking sheet in the oven and preheat to 190°C/375°F/Gas 5. Peel the pears, halve them, remove the cores and rub with lemon juice. Put the pear halves cut side down on a board and slice thinly crossways, keeping the slices together.

3 ▲ Pour the almond cream filling into the pastry case. Slide a palette knife under one pear half and press the top with your fingers to fan out the slices. Transfer to the tart, placing the fruit on the filling like spokes of a wheel. If you like, remove a few slices from each half before arranging and use to fill in any gaps in the centre.

4 Place the tart on the hot baking sheet and bake for 50–55 minutes, or until the filling is set and well browned. Cool on a wire rack.

5 ▼ Meanwhile, heat the brandy or water and the preserve in a small pan, then brush over the top of the hot tart to glaze. Serve the tart at room temperature.

# DESSERTS

Simple and wholesome home-made desserts are the hallmark of country cooking. They are usually made from local ingredients – apples in Normandy, cherries in the central regions, peaches and pears further south, and prunes from Agen, in the southwest. In French homes, especially in the country, weekday desserts are often nothing fancier than fresh fruit and cheese, but family occasions and other celebrations provide the opportunity for more festive fare – custards or crêpes perhaps, or an apple charlotte. These kinds of traditional rustic desserts prepared in family kitchens and provincial restaurants are wonderfully satisfying and appealing in their simplicity.

# CHERRY BATTER PUDDING *Clafoutis aux Cerises*

*This dessert originated in the Limousin area of central France, where batters play an important role in the hearty cuisine. Similar fruit and custard desserts are found in Alsace.*

SERVES 4

*450g/1lb ripe cherries*
*30ml/2 tbsp Kirsch or fruit brandy or 15ml/1 tbsp lemon juice*
*15ml/1 tbsp icing (confectioners') sugar*
*30g/1oz/3 tbsp plain (all-purpose) flour*
*45ml/3 tbsp granulated sugar*
*175ml/6fl oz/¾ cup milk or single (light) cream*
*2 eggs*
*grated rind of ½ lemon*
*pinch of freshly grated nutmeg*
*1.5ml/¼ tsp vanilla essence (extract)*

1 ▼ Stone (pit) the cherries if you like, then mix them with the Kirsch, brandy or lemon juice and icing sugar and set aside for 1–2 hours.

2 ▲ Preheat the oven to 190°C/375°F/Gas 5. Generously butter a 28cm/11in oval gratin dish or other shallow ovenproof dish.

3 ▲ Sift the flour into a bowl, add the sugar and slowly whisk in the milk until smoothly blended. Add the eggs, lemon rind, nutmeg and vanilla essence and whisk until well combined and smooth.

4 ▲ Sprinkle the cherries evenly in the baking dish. Pour over the batter and bake for 45 minutes, or until set and puffed around the edges. A knife inserted in the centre should come out clean. Serve warm or at room temperature.

# APPLE CHARLOTTE

*Charlotte aux Pommes*

*This classic dessert takes its name from the straight-sided tin with heart-shaped handles in which it is baked. The buttery bread crust encases a thick and sweet yet sharp apple purée.*

SERVES 6

*1.2kg/2½lb apples*
*30ml/2 tbsp water*
*120g/4oz/⅔ cup soft light brown sugar*
*2.5ml/½ tsp ground cinnamon*
*1.5ml/¼ tsp freshly grated nutmeg*
*7 slices firm textured sliced white bread*
*70–85g/2½-3oz/5–6 tbsp butter, melted*
*custard, to serve (optional)*

1 ▲ Peel, quarter and core the apples. Cut into thick slices and put in a large heavy pan with the water. Cook, covered, over a medium-low heat for 5 minutes, and then uncover the pan and cook for 10 minutes until the apples are very soft. Add the sugar, cinnamon and nutmeg and continue cooking for 5–10 minutes, stirring frequently, until the apples are soft and thick. (There should be about 750ml/1¼ pints/3 cups of apple purée.)

COOK'S TIP

If preferred, microwave the apples without water in a large glass dish at High (100% power), tightly covered, for 15 minutes. Add the sugar and spices and microwave, uncovered, for about 15 minutes more until very thick, stirring once or twice.

2 ▼ Preheat the oven to 200°C/400°F/Gas 6. Trim the crusts from the bread and brush with melted butter on one side. Cut two slices into triangles and use as many as necessary to cover the base of a 1.4 litre/2¼ pint/6 cup charlotte tin (pan) or soufflé dish, placing them buttered-sides down and fitting them tightly. Cut fingers of bread the same height as the tin or dish and use them to completely line the sides, overlapping them slightly.

3 ▲ Pour the apple purée into the tin or dish. Cover the top with bread slices, buttered-side up, cutting them as necessary to fit.

4 Bake the charlotte for 20 minutes, then reduce the oven temperature to 180°C/350°F/Gas 4 and bake for 25 minutes until well browned and firm. Leave to stand for 15 minutes. To turn out, place a serving plate over the tin or dish, hold tightly, and invert, then lift off the tin or dish. Serve with custard if wished.

# CRÊPES WITH ORANGE SAUCE *Crêpes Suzette*

*This is one of the best-known French desserts and is easy to do at home. You can make the crêpes in advance, then you will be able to put the dish together quickly at the last minute.*

SERVES 6

*120g/4oz/⅔ cup plain (all-purpose) flour*
*1.5ml/¼ tsp salt*
*30g/1oz/2 tbsp caster (superfine) sugar*
*2 eggs, lightly beaten*
*250ml/8fl oz/1 cup milk*
*60ml/4 tbsp water*
*30ml/2 tbsp orange flower water or orange liqueur (optional)*
*30g/1oz/2 tbsp unsalted (sweet) butter, melted, plus more for frying*

FOR THE ORANGE SAUCE

*85g/3oz/6 tbsp unsalted (sweet) butter*
*55g/2oz/¼ cup caster (superfine) sugar*
*grated rind and juice of 1 large unwaxed orange*
*grated rind and juice of 1 unwaxed lemon*
*150ml/¼ pint/⅔ cup fresh orange juice*
*60ml/4 tbsp orange liqueur, plus extra for flaming (optional)*
*brandy, for flaming (optional)*
*orange segments, to decorate*

1 ▲ In a medium bowl, sift together the flour, salt and sugar. Make a well in the centre and pour in the eggs. Using an electric whisk, beat the eggs, bringing in a little flour until it is all incorporated. Slowly whisk in the milk and water to make a smooth batter. Whisk in the orange flower water or liqueur, if using, then strain the batter into a large jug (pitcher) and set aside for 20–30 minutes. If the batter thickens, thin it with a little milk or water.

2 ▲ Heat a 18–20cm/7–8in crêpe pan (preferably non-stick) over a medium heat. Stir the melted butter into the crêpe batter. Brush the hot pan with a little extra melted butter and pour in about 30ml/2 tbsp of batter. Quickly tilt and rotate the pan to cover the base with a thin layer of batter. Cook for about 1 minute until the top is set and the base is golden. With a palette knife or metal spatula, lift the edge to check the colour, then carefully turn over the crêpe and cook for 20–30 seconds. Tip out on to a plate.

3 ▲ Continue cooking the crêpes, stirring the batter occasionally and brushing the pan with a little melted butter as and when necessary. Place a sheet of clear film (plastic wrap) between the crêpes as they are stacked to prevent sticking. (Crêpes can be prepared ahead to this point – wrap and chill until ready to use.)

4 To make the sauce, melt the butter in a large frying pan over a medium-low heat, then stir in the sugar, orange and lemon rind and juice, the additional orange juice and the orange liqueur.

5 ▲ Place a crêpe in the pan browned-side down, swirling gently to coat with the sauce. Fold it in half, then in half again to form a triangle and push to the side of the pan. Continue heating and folding the crêpes until all are warm and covered with the sauce.

6 ▲ To flame the crêpes, heat 30–45ml/2–3 tbsp each of orange liqueur and brandy in a small pan over a medium heat. Remove the pan from the heat, carefully ignite the liquid with a match then gently pour over the crêpes. Sprinkle over the orange segments and serve immediately.

# BAKED CARAMEL CUSTARD *Crème Caramel*

*Also called* crème renversée, *this is one of the most popular French desserts and is wonderful when freshly made. This is a slightly lighter version of the traditional recipe.*

SERVES 6–8

*250g/9oz/1¼ cups granulated sugar*
*60ml/4 tbsp water*
*1 vanilla pod (bean) or 10ml/2 tsp vanilla essence (extract)*
*425ml/14fl oz/1¾ cups milk*
*250ml/8fl oz/1 cup whipping cream*
*5 large eggs*
*2 egg yolks*

1 Put 175g/6oz/⅞ cup of the sugar in a small heavy pan with the water to moisten. Bring to the boil over a high heat, swirling the pan to dissolve the sugar. Boil, without stirring, until the syrup turns a dark caramel colour (this will take about 4–5 minutes).

2 ▼ Immediately pour the caramel into a 1 litre/1⅔ pint/4 cup soufflé dish. Holding the dish with oven gloves, quickly swirl the dish to coat the base and sides with the caramel and set aside. (The caramel will harden quickly as it cools.) Place the dish in a small roasting pan.

3 ▲ Preheat the oven to 170°C/325°F/Gas 3. With a small sharp knife, carefully split the vanilla pod lengthways and scrape the black seeds into a medium pan. Add the milk and cream and bring just to the boil over a medium-high heat, stirring frequently. Remove the pan from the heat, cover and set aside for 15–20 minutes.

4 In a bowl, whisk the eggs and egg yolks with the remaining sugar for 2–3 minutes until smooth and creamy. Whisk in the hot milk and carefully strain the mixture into the caramel-lined dish. Cover with foil.

5 Place the dish in a roasting pan and pour in enough boiling water to come halfway up the sides of the dish. Bake the custard for 40–45 minutes until a knife inserted about 5cm/2in from the edge comes out clean (the custard should be just set). Remove from the roasting pan and cool for at least ½ hour, then chill overnight.

6 To turn out, carefully run a sharp knife around the edge of the dish to loosen the custard. Cover the dish with a serving plate and holding them tightly, invert the dish and plate together. Gently lift one edge of the dish, allowing the caramel to run over the sides, then slowly lift off the dish.

# Chocolate Profiteroles

## *Profiteroles au Chocolat*

*This mouth-watering dessert is served in cafés throughout France. Sometimes the profiteroles are filled with whipped cream instead of ice cream, but they are always drizzled with chocolate sauce.*

Serves 4–6

*275g/10oz plain (semisweet) chocolate*
*120ml/8 tbsp warm water*
*750ml/1¼ pints/3 cups vanilla ice cream*
For the profiteroles
*110g/3¾oz/¾ cup plain (all-purpose) flour*
*1.5ml/¼ tsp salt*
*pinch of freshly grated nutmeg*
*175ml/6fl oz/¾ cup water*
*85g/3oz/6 tbsp unsalted (sweet) butter, cut into 6 pieces*
*3 eggs*

1 Preheat the oven to 200°C/400°F/Gas 6 and butter a baking sheet.

2 To make the profiteroles, sift together the flour, salt and nutmeg. In a medium pan, bring the water and butter to the boil. Remove from the heat and add the dry ingredients all at once. Beat with a wooden spoon for about 1 minute until well blended and the mixture starts to pull away from the sides of the pan, then set the pan over a low heat and cook the mixture for about 2 minutes, beating constantly. Remove from the heat.

3 ▲ Beat 1 egg in a small bowl and set aside. Add the remaining eggs, one at a time, to the flour mixture, beating well after each. Add the beaten egg by teaspoonfuls until the dough is smooth and shiny; it should pull away and fall slowly when dropped from a spoon.

4 ▼ Using a tablespoon, drop the dough on to the baking sheet in 12 mounds. Bake for 25–30 minutes until the pastry is well risen and browned. Turn off the oven and leave the puffs to cool with the oven door open.

5 To make the sauce, place the chocolate and water in a double-boiler or in a bowl placed over a pan of hot water and leave to melt, stirring occasionally. Keep warm until ready to serve, or reheat, over simmering water.

6 Split the profiteroles in half and put a small scoop of ice cream in each. Arrange on a serving platter or divide among individual plates. Pour the chocolate sauce over the top and serve immediately.

## GINGER BAKED PEARS *Poires au Gingembre*

*This simple dessert is the kind that would be served after Sunday lunch or a family supper. Try to find Comice or Anjou pears – the recipe is especially useful for slightly under-ripe fruit.*

SERVES 4

*4 large pears*
*300ml/½ pint/1¼ cups whipping cream*
*55g/2oz/¼ cup caster (superfine) sugar*
*2.5ml/½ tsp vanilla essence (extract)*
*1.5ml/¼ tsp ground cinnamon*
*pinch of freshly grated nutmeg*
*5ml/1 tsp grated fresh root ginger*

VARIATION

If preferred, you could substitute about 30ml/1 tbsp finely chopped preserved stem ginger for the fresh root ginger and add a little of the ginger syrup to the cream.

1 Preheat the oven to 190°C/375°F/Gas 5. Lightly butter a large shallow baking dish.

2 ▼ Peel the pears, cut in half lengthways and remove the cores. Arrange, cut-sides down, in a single layer in the baking dish.

3 ▲ Mix together the cream, sugar, vanilla essence, cinnamon, nutmeg and ginger and pour over the pears.

4 Bake for 30–35 minutes, basting from time to time, until the pears are tender and browned on top and the cream is thick and bubbly. Cool slightly before serving.

## PRUNES POACHED IN RED WINE *Compôte de Pruneaux Agennaise*

*Serve this simple dessert on its own, or with crème fraîche or vanilla ice cream. The most delicious plump prunes come from the orchards around Agen in South-west France.*

SERVES 8–10

*1 unwaxed orange*
*1 unwaxed lemon*
*750ml/1¼ pints/3 cups fruity red wine*
*500ml/16fl oz/2 cups water*
*55g/2oz/¼ cup caster (superfine) sugar, or to taste*
*1 cinnamon stick*
*pinch of freshly grated nutmeg*
*2 or 3 cloves*
*5ml/1 tsp black peppercorns*
*1 bay leaf*
*900g/2lb large stoned (pitted) prunes, soaked in cold water*
*strips of orange rind, to decorate*

1 Using a vegetable peeler, peel two or three strips of rind from both the orange and lemon. Squeeze the juice from both and put in a large pan.

2 Add the wine, water, sugar, spices, peppercorns, bay leaf and strips of rind to the pan.

3 ▲ Bring to the boil over a medium heat, stirring occasionally to dissolve the sugar. Drain the prunes and add to the pan, reduce the heat to low and simmer, covered, for 10–15 minutes until tender. Remove from the heat and set aside until cool.

4 ▼ Using a slotted spoon, transfer the prunes to a serving dish. Return the cooking liquid to a medium-high heat and bring to the boil. Boil for 5–10 minutes until slightly reduced and syrupy, then pour or strain over the prunes. Cool, then chill before serving, decorated with strips of orange rind, if you like.

# Glossary

*The following terms are frequently used in French cooking. In the recipes we have tried to reduce the use of technical terms by describing the procedures, but understanding these words is helpful.*

BAIN-MARIE: a baking tin (pan) or dish set in a pan or roasting pan of water. It allows the food to cook indirectly and protects delicate foods; a double boiler is also a kind of water bath, or *bain-marie.*

BAKE BLIND: to bake or partially bake a pastry case before adding a filling, usually done to prevent the filling making the pastry soggy.

BASTE: to moisten food with fat or cooking juices while it is cooking.

BEURRE MANIÉ: equal parts of butter and flour blended to a paste and whisked into simmering cooking liquid for thickening after cooking is completed.

BLANCH: to immerse vegetables and sometimes fruit in boiling water in order to loosen skin, remove bitterness or saltiness or preserve colour.

BOIL: to keep liquid at a temperature producing bubbles that break the surface.

BOUQUET GARNI: a bunch of herbs, usually including a bay leaf, thyme sprigs and parsley stalks, used to impart flavour during cooking, often tied for easy removal.

CLARIFY: to make an opaque liquid clear and remove impurities; stocks are clarified using egg white, butter by skimming.

COULIS: a purée, usually fruit or vegetable, sometimes sweetened or flavoured with herbs, but not thickened, used as a sauce.

CROÛTONS: small crisp pieces of fried or baked crustless bread.

DEGLAZE: to dissolve the sediment from the bottom of a cooking pan by adding liquid and bringing to the boil, stirring. This is then used as the basis for a sauce or gravy.

DEGREASE: to remove fat from cooking liquid, either by spooning off after it has risen to the top or by chilling until the fat is congealed and lifting it off.

DICE: to cut food into square uniform pieces about 5mm/¼in.

EMULSIFY: to combine two usually incompatible ingredients until smooth by mixing rapidly while slowly adding one to the other so they are held in suspension.

FOLD: to combine ingredients, using a large rubber spatula or metal spoon, by cutting down through the centre of the bowl, then along the side and up to the top in a semicircular motion; it is important not to deflate or over-work ingredients while folding.

FOOD MILL *(mouli-légumes)*: tool for puréeing found in most French kitchens which strains as it purées.

GLAZE: to coat food with a sweet or savoury mixture producing a shiny surface when set.

GRATINÉ: to give a browned, crisp surface to a baked dish.

HERBES DE PROVENCE: a mixture of aromatic dried herbs, which grow wild in Provence, usually thyme, marjoram, oregano and summer savory.

INFUSE: to extract flavour by steeping in hot liquid.

JULIENNE: thin matchstick pieces of vegetables, fruit or other food.

MACERATE: to bathe fruit in liquid to soften and flavour it.

PAPILLOTE: a greased baking parchment or foil parcel, traditionally heart-shaped, enclosing food for cooking.

PAR-BOIL: to partially cook food by boiling.

POACH: to cook food, submerged in liquid, by gentle simmering.

REDUCE: to boil a liquid for the purpose of concentrating the flavour by evaporation.

ROUX: a cooked mixture of fat and flour used to thicken liquids such as soups, stews and sauces.

SAUTÉ: to fry quickly in a small amount of fat over a high heat.

SCALD: to heat liquid, usually milk, until bubbles begin to form around the edge.

SCORE: to make shallow incisions to aid penetration of heat or liquid or for decoration.

SIMMER: to keep a liquid at just below boiling point so the liquid just trembles.

SKIM: to remove froth or scum from the surface of stocks etc.

STEAM: moist heat cooking method by which vaporized liquid cooks food in a closed container.

SWEAT: to cook gently in fat, covered, so liquid in ingredients is rendered to steam them.

# INDEX

A TRINQUELINETTE